Dressage Dreams **10**

Dressage Dreams 10

Stephen Clarke

LH

Dressage Dreams 10

Created and designed by
LewisHarding Ltd
Ditchells Farm House
Delmonden Lane
Hawkhurst, Kent TN18 4XB
Tel: +44(0)1580 752346
www.lewisharding.com
www.lewisharding.co.uk

First published in Great Britain 2009
by LewisHarding

ISBN: 978 0 9563259 0 7

A CIP record for this book is available from the British
Library

Set in Fairfield LT Light and Bliss

Colour origination by Rival Colour, London
Printed and bound by Printer Trento, Italy, using pulp from
sustainable forests.

Author: Stephen Clarke
Managing/Commission Editor: Valerie Lewis
Head of Photography: Paul Harding
Production: Angela Young
Editorial: Ann-Marie Mullen, Alexandra Wortley, Fiona
Brenninkmeijer, Harriet Lewis, Jane Kidd
Design: Mark Winwood
Indexer: Hilary Bird
Sales and Marketing: Inigo Brenninkmeijer

Jacket photographs: Front - Moorlands Totilas and Edward Gal with
kind permission from Tosca and Kees Visser, Back - Fuego XII and
Juan Manuel Munoz Diaz, Flap - Deinhard B and Going East.

Photo: Scoreboard at The European Chamionships, Windsor

Photo: Anky van Grunsven and Salinero, Windsor

Acknowledgements

The publisher and author of *Dressage Dreams* would like to acknowledge the great assistance given by the press officers and their staff at the many show venues we visited.

CDI-W Odense JBK Horse Shows Aps, Bedervej 101, DK-8320 Maarslet, Denmark.

CDI-W Frankfurt Frankfurter Reit- und Turnierstall, Schwarz-Gelb e.V in cooperation with ESCON-International GmbH, Europa-Allee 12, D-49685 Emstek, Germany.

CDI-W Olympia HorsePower International, Stable House, St Albans Close, SL4 1UT Windsor, Berkshire Media Officer Candy Burnyeat.

CDI-W 's Hertzenbosh Stichting International Concours, Hippique, Indoor Brabant, 5202 CA 's-Hertogenbosh, Netherlands. Press Officer Gerrit Jan Swinkels.

CHIO Rotterdam Kralingseweg 120, 3006 AG Rotterdam, Press Officer Ms Anita Lussenburg.

Aachen CHIO Aachen-Laurensberger Rennverein e.V., Office Press & Public Relations, Albert-Servais-Allee 50, 52070 Aachen, Germany, Press Mr Niels Knippertz.

CDI Hartpury Hartpury College, Hartpury, Gloucestershire, GL19 3BE Press Officer Ms Janet Plant.

Pony Europeans Championships (2009) Avenches, Switzerland.

Hickstead CDIO Bolney Park Farm, Broxmead Lane, Bolney, West Sussex RH17 5RJ, Press Officer Mrs Marie Mepham.

CDI Stuttgart German Dressage Masters, Veranstaltungsgesellschaft, Mercedesstrabe 50, 70372 Stuttgart, Press Officer Jörg Klopfer.

Windsor European Dressage Championships HorsePower International, Stable House, St Albans Close, SL4 1UT Windsor, Berkshire Media Officer Candy Burnyeat.

CDI-W Stockholm, Swedish Equestrian Federation and Stockholm Globe Arena AB, 121 27 Stockholm. Press Officer Lotta Amnestal.

Photographers' Acknowledgements

The following talented photographers have supplied LewisHarding with the most beautiful illustrations to demonstrate the power, elegance and athleticism of horse and rider in action.

1 **Paul Harding**, UK, Director of Photography for LewisHarding studied as a medical photographer. Although interest in other business pursuits delayed a career in photography he has now built up a sizeable library with a focus on all aspects of international equine sport. With a passion for writing, travel and photography he can be found at most FEI events. www.lewisharding.com

2 **Kevin Sparrow**, UK, has been photographing horses since 1989, from the most elite sports horses in the world to the most loved. His speciality is recording that ephemeral moment that captures the true spirit and beauty of the horse and moments of sporting history. Kevin's work frequently appears in *Horse and Hound*, *British Dressage* magazine and other leading publications in the UK and abroad. www.kevinsparrow.co.uk

3 **Arnd Bronkhorst** NL, was exposed to horses at an early age but it was not until he was in his thirties that he began to photograph them professionally. Having studied photography at the Royal Arts Academy in The Hague he then began working for the top Dutch Horse magazines as well as developing his reputation on the international competition scene in all disciplines of equestrian sport. www.arnd.nl

4 **Dirk Caremans** Bel, inherited his passion for photography and art from his father, who is a passionate amateur landscape painter. He is an expert in indoor photography and travels to all the European dressage and show jumping competitions as

9

well as international shows in the US and Australia. His pictures appear in many equestrian books and magazines. www.hippofoto.be

5 **Astrid Appels** Bel, creator, designer and editor of the very useful and informative website www.eurodressage.com. Her love of horses began at a very young age and despite the demands of obtaining a Phd in English Literature she has managed to cover every major dressage competition and breeding show in Europe for the past decade.

6 **Jan Gyllensten** SWE, has spent more than 30 years photographing horses and equestrian sport around the world. His photo archive has grown subsequently into one of the largest in the equestrian world with many of his images used in the leading equestrian magazines throughout the world. Jan also has a personal interest in dogs. www.photogyllensten.com

7 **Barbara Schnell** GER, is not only a photographer of equestrian subjects but she also has a passion for landscapes, dogs and people. Her pictures have graced the covers of many German horse magazines. She is also a translator, a journalist and author. www.bschnell.de

8 **Jacques Toffi** was born in Syria and he obtained a Bachelor's degree from a German school in Beirut before moving to Germany in 1970 where he obtained a license as a Sea Captain. He always had a passion for photography and finally became a professional photographer in 1984 and is now one of the industry's finest. His subjects include most equestrian sports, still life and portraits www.toffi-images.de

Jorgen Bak Rasmussen (no photo available) is a Danish publisher, electrician among other professions who started a small photographic company over 10 years ago. He now publishes several magazines on the subject of horses and dogs for his own company and for other clients. www.wiegaarden.dk

9 **Werner and Tammo Ernst** GER, father and son business with a photo library dating from 1968 the Ernsts have attended every major equestrian event. Their speciality is breeder posing shots and their images fill the catalogues of major horse auctions in Europe. www.pferdebild.de

Maximilian Schreiner (no photo available) is a professional photographers who for many years has worked for trade magazines as well as breeders, dealers, lovers of horses from international, national and regional areas of the horse scene. His pictures have appeared in most German-language journals and magazines. www.im-blickpunkt.com.

10 **Mary Phelps** USA is the creator of the equine websites www.Horsedaily.com and www.PhelpsPhotos.com, a specialist agent for horse insurance and an accomplished equine photographer. Established in 1997 Mary's coverage of equine events in the United States is second to none.

Pelle Wahlgren (no photo available) SWE, is not only a fabulous equestrian photographer but also know in Sweden for his still-life photography. He travels the world searching for subjects in their natural habitat working both for himself and commissions from clients. www.studiowahlgren.com

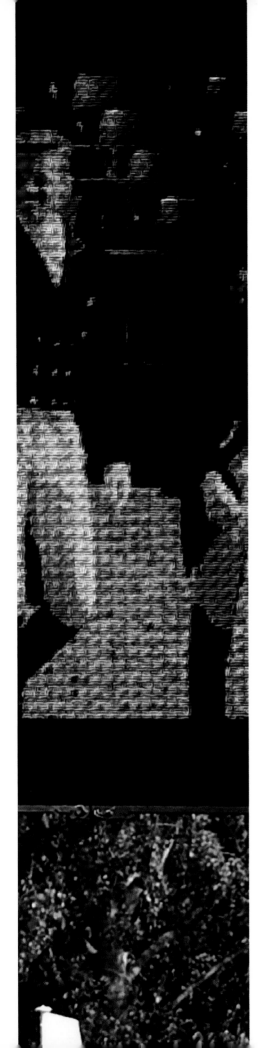

Contents

Photo: Winners of the Grand Prix Special, Windsor 2009

Photo: The judges box at Aachen

Foreword

This wonderful book, *Dressage Dreams*, reflects the true character of Stephen Clarke. When I heard that Stephen was writing this book, I was sure it would be written in Stephen's very positive style - and it is.

In 1991, when I was Chairman of the FEI Dressage Committee, Stephen attended one of my first Judges Courses which was held at Hickstead. At that time England needed more International Judges and I encouraged and supported Stephen in this direction. I did not have to do much because in no time at all Stephen had become accepted and respected by riders, trainers and show organizers. In a very short time he became an FEI O-judge (the highest level obtainable) due mainly to his deep knowledge of the sport and his positive way of judging and dealing with people. Always humble and polite but also with absolute integrity, he has been judging for some time and now gives Judges Courses throughout the World. Stephen has judged all the major dressage events including the Olympic Games and many World Cup Finals. He has really stood by and lived up to his positive judging ethos, which I feel is the best way to bring our sport forward . . . 'Search for the good things and observe the faults'.

Dressage at it's best can be thought of as an art form. Over the years dressage has improved because breeders are breeding horses for today's sport and no longer for the army. It has taken generations of good breeding practice to produce the fantastic horses we now have. A good dressage horse is a talented horse that through correct training can achieve high marks from the judges. To make dressage even better it is not only about reducing the mistakes, but to develop the talent of the horse.

Stephen has written this book because he loves good dressage and beautiful horses. He has, like other top judges, seen the best horses and riders from the best position, i.e. five meters away from the arena, in the judges' box. It has been a privilege for me to have judged at many shows together with Stephen. He is always dreaming of giving the mark for excellence '10', because all involved within the sport can recognise excellence. You do not have to be an expert to be impressed and enjoy good dressage.

Eric Lette

Photo: World Cup Qualifier, Frankfurt 2007

Introduction

It was well over a year ago that I first met with the editor of *Dressage Dreams* in London to discuss the feasibility of doing this book. It doesn't seem possible that is it now published. Since that time so much has happened in the Dressage world - retirements of top horses and riders, challenges to the system, new talent bursting onto the scene like never before - who said dressage was boring.

Over the last two decades we have seen the sport of Dressage transform it's image and develop itself from a relatively non-commercial entity into a 'must attend' sporting event. The inclusion of the Kur in all major championships is largely responsible for bringing dressage from a learned discipline to a great entertainment sport that anyone who can appreciate the magical harmony between horse and rider will want to see. Dressage attendance at European Championships, World Games and World Cup Finals is rocketing. In Germany alone more people attended the weekend of the World Equestrian Games than attended the Formula 1 Motor Racing Grand Prix. Over the past years Germany and Holland have traditionally been the powerhouses of the sport. But the fever is spreading! Countries that in previous years could only field one or two top international calibre riders are now able to produce really competitive teams.

With the growth in interest should also come the commercial backing for the sport. We already have some fabulous benefactors but, in comparison to other sports, dressage still needs greater sponsorship for the top ranking shows - sponsorship which is so important in order to encourage the top horses and riders to travel the distances necessary to be competitive on the world stage. Attendance figures are climbing and those industries associated with dressage are finding a focused audience to expose their wares to.

In my role as a Dressage Judge it has been fascinating to officiate in many countries around the world and to witness, on virtually an annual basis, the improvements of standards globally.

Dressage has also seen an emergence of talent like never before. The medal table at Championship level used to be a fairly predictable affair, but over the last couple of years we have seen some fresh faces come up and produce the goods that have altered the status quo. This is of course very healthy for the sport and proves that if anyone is good enough, they can win.

The biggest problem in the development of this book was deciding who to choose to demonstrate the movements, when there are so many able partnerships. And then to decide which partnerships to use to demonstrate which movements, when in reality all of the subjects chosen were capable of, or have achieved 10s in most of the Grand Prix movements.

I would like to thank all the riders and trainers who agreed to be in *Dressage Dreams* and for their time and patience in supplying us with information about themselves when in the arena and behind the scenes. I would also like to thank the many photographers who searched back in their archives to supply us with suitable pictures of our heroes who performed before digital cameras were used.

I hope you enjoy this brief insight into the lives and moments of some of these wonderful horses and riders who are directly responsible for uplifting our sport and bringing us all so much excitement and pleasure.

Stephen Clarke

History of Competitive Dressage

Dressage, the highest expression of horse training, is considered to be the art of equestrian sport and is used as the groundwork for all the other disciplines. Its beginnings can be traced back to the 17th century courts of Renaissance Europe and today, interest in dressage continues to grow throughout the world as a sport and a pastime. Dressage is also one of the three disciplines in competition at the Olympic Games, the other two being Jumping and Eventing.

The long and colourful traditions of Dressage go as far back as ancient Greece: the first known work on horsemanship dealing with Dressage was written by the general Xenophon (430 – 354 BC) who is considered the founder of the discipline. With the disintegration of ancient Greece, the art of riding slowly fell into oblivion and was not revived until the Italian Renaissance in the 16th century. A riding academy was created in Naples in 1532, the teachings of which gradually reached Baroque France. *Le Manège Royal*, written in 1632, concentrated on understanding the character of the horse and winning its co-operation.

In the 18th century classical Dressage reached its peak with the creation of the world-famous Spanish Riding School in 1729 in Vienna, which laid the basis of the modern discipline.

Despite the fact that over the centuries the discipline had enjoyed numerous followers and theorists, the first competition was not held until 1873 in Vienna, Austria. The first international competition took place in Turin, Italy, in 1902. Dressage events were part of the 1912 Olympic Games in Stockholm, when equestrianism made its Olympic debut.

The first FEI Dressage championship outside the Olympic Games was held in 1930 at Lucerne, Switzerland. The first FEI World Championship was held in Bern, Switzerland.

In modern competitions, horse and rider are expected to perform, from memory, a series of predetermined movements, known as figures (volte, serpentine, figure of eight). The completely flat arena, measuring 60 x 20 metres, is skirted by a low rail along which 12 lettered markers are placed symmetrically indicating where movements are to start, where changes of pace or lead are to occur and where the movements are to end. In all competitions, the horse has to show three paces: walk, trot and canter, as well as smooth transitions within and between these paces.

A high quality test is revealed by the freedom and regularity of the horses paces, lightness and ease of the movements. The horse gives the impression of doing the movements of his own accord and shows immediate and even intuitive response to the rider's commands.

At international competitions regulated by the FEI, horse and rider combinations are expected to perform the following tests:
• Prix St-Georges (of medium standard)
• Intermediate 1 (of relatively advanced standard)
• Intermediate 2 (of advanced standard)
• Grand Prix is a highly demanding test of over five-and-a-half-minutes, requiring all of the basic schooling movements plus the fundamental airs of the Classical High School, including pirouettes (pivots on the spot at a prescribed gait), piaffe, passage and flying lead changes.
• Grand Prix Special is a seven minute test requiring the same movements as the Grand Prix but in a different order and with increased focus on the more advanced movements
• Grand Prix Freestyle (Kür) is performed to the accompaniment of a musical score. Most of the marks, based on purity of action, rhythm and regularity, impulsion and collection, are for technical performance. Some of the most spectacular Dressage performances occur during the Kür which are often tailor-made for the performance.

The standard formula for FEI world and continental

championships and the Olympic Games consists of Grand Prix, Grand Prix Special and Grand Prix Freestyle (Kür) tests. The Grand Prix test decides the team medals and serves as a first individual qualifying round. The top 18 to 25 riders (the number varies depending on the type of competition) progress to the more demanding Grand Prix Special. The best riders, based on total points from the two previous tests, qualify for the medal round where they perform a Grand Prix Freestyle (Kür) test.

The Premier Dressage Competitions are:
Olympic Games
The Olympic Games take place every 4 years. Dressage events were part of the 1912 Olympics in Stockholm, when equestrianism made its Olympic debut.

FEI World Equestrian Games
The FEI World Equestrian Games (WEG) are held every 4 years in the even years between the Olympics.

FEI World Cup™ Dressage
Initiated in 1986, the FEI World Cup™ Dressage is the only annual worldwide linked series in this discipline. It consists of a series of qualifying leagues encompassing Western and Central Europe, North America, Canada and Australia. Each FEI World Cup™ qualifier comprises a Grand Prix test, which in turn is a qualification for the Freestyle to Music competition, where league points are accumulated towards places in the FEI World Cup™ Dressage Final.

Continental Championships
Continental and Regional Games organized under the patronage of the International Olympic Committee and Regional Games Associations.

The first official Freestyle to Music competition was launched with the FEI World Cup™ Dressage series. This prepared the way for the introduction of the freestyle into the Olympic, World and European Championship formats. Judged on both technical and artistic merit, the FEI World Cup™ Dressage combines art, sport and partnership between horse and rider at the highest level and consistently proves a winning formula with audiences all over the world. The FEI

World Cup™ series culminates in a yearly final.

Most top dressage horses are at least 10 years old because it takes that long to train them to the most advanced level. Attributes such as carriage, paces, character, willingness to work and an outstanding learning ability are part of the equation. 'When you lose a horse in Dressage, you lose a friend, a partner. It's a catastrophe,' says renowned rider, Anky van Grunsven.

Scoring A panel of five judges assess each of the figures awarding a mark from 1 to 10. Once totalled, these scores produce a percentage and the rider or team with the highest total score is declared the winner.

Equipment Formal dress, consisting of top hat, tails, white shirt and tie, gloves, white or cream breeches and black boots, is compulsory. Members of the armed and police forces wear uniforms.

Information kindly supplied by the FEI
Photo: Monica Theodorescu and Whisper

Lightness

Carl Hester and Escapado

True lightness is the end result of the development of all the elements of the scales of training: rhythm, suppleness, contact, impulsion, straightness and collection. Only when the horse is working '*through*' the body (*durchlassigkeit*) with the energy coming from the hind quarters, through a supple and swinging back, into an elastic and accepting contact with the bit, can the *pushing power* of the hind legs be transformed, by the influence of the half-halt, into *carrying power* that manifests itself into a state of lightness both within the footfalls and the carriage of the horse.

Carl Hester is Britain's best known rider. He is respected and admired worldwide for having his innate ability to bring out the very best in such a huge variety of horses. With each and every one of the horses he trains he stamps his trademark of energy and lightness. Never in either the warm up areas or in the test itself, does he ever appear to use strength or force. He doesn't need to, his instinctive feel and lightening quick response to each horse's thought and deed enables him to always seem to be one step ahead of any possible argument or mishap.

Seen here with the elegant, but sometimes volatile, Escapado, at the Athens Olympic Games when the horse was still a relatively inexperienced Grand Prix campaigner, again the most impressive quality that hits the eye, is this lightness of Escapado's carriage and footfalls. One is given the impression that if the horse was performing on concrete instead of the rather beautiful footing of the Athens arena, you would not even hear his feet touching the ground. Of course this lightness originates from the lively impulsion that comes from the highly developed engagement of the hindquarters and the fingertip response to the rider's half halt that can then produce the horse in such an ideal balance and carriage.

Carl's elegant and perfectly balanced position in the saddle is again the key factor in his ability to ride with such light but effective hand and leg aids that can, when necessary, produce an instant and electric reaction. It is this lightning quick response that Carl manages to get from each horse he rides by just using the subtlest of aids that is the hallmark of his training and no doubt has contributed to his amazing record of winning over fifty National dressage titles in Great Britain on almost as many different horses. These titles cover a wide range of British dressage levels from Novice to Grand Prix. Carl's personality, talent and enthusiasm for the sport has done so much for the promotion of dressage and made him somewhat of a icon in Great Britain. His strong following is made up inspired young riders who want to be just like him to more professional riders who want to learn from him.

The bittersweet partnership between Carl and Escapado ended in 2005 when Escapado was sold to the Dutch sponsor and promoter of World Dressage Masters, Exquis, with Hans Peter Minderhoud taking over the ride. Hans Peter's amazing talent and understanding of Escapado ment this new partnership have been able to continue to enjoy a highly successful dressage career at the Grand Prix level.

Carl Hester

The Rider

My most memorable test

The Grand Prix Special at the 2005 European Championships at Hagen Germany was where it all came together for me and Escapado. For us to get that far was a long journey, one that I was never certain of the outcome. In 2003 after a very successful competition year I realised what a superstar Escapado was becoming so I made the commitment to him that I would work even harder to prepare us for the selection trials for the 2004 Athens Olympics. We achieved our dream and represented Great Britain at the Games. We did not win a medal but we were the highest scoring British combination there. Feeling very inspired we set our sights on qualifiying for the World Cup Finals in Las Vegas the following year, which we did coming 9th in the Grand Prix and 10th in the Kur. I felt we were improving so much that I then wanted us to try for the European Championships. My trainer Anna van Olst was behind me all the way.

Escapado and I spent lots of time at her farm in Holland and every day with Anna's training I felt we just got better and better. Anna knew that I had already sold Escapado to Hans Peter Minderhoud and the Europeans would be my last ride on him, so she really wanted us to go for it - to go out on top. At the Europeans Escapado was amazing. The commitment had worked, everything had worked - he was awesome to ride and he did a brilliant Grand Prix.

Escapado can be very unpredictable sometimes and even as we were going into the arena that day, my fingers were crossed and I was thinking - will he settle? But the half-passes were big, the piaffe passage transitions smooth, the harmony solid and he remained

Above Carl Hester after winning the CDI Intermediaire I on Movistar, a KWPN stallion by Jazz, at Hartpury Equestrian College in Gloucestershire
Opposite, right Carl Hester in a publicity shot with the other British Team members selected for the 2004 Athens Olympics l. to r. Richard Davison, Emma Hindle, Chef d'Equipe David Trott, Nicola McGivern and Carl

My Story

1967 I was born on the 29th June on the Isle of Sark.

1985 I left Sark to pursue an equestrian career on mainland England and became National Dressage Young Rider Champion.

1990 Participated in my first International as a member of the British team.

1996/7 Won Dressage Trainer of the year and Spillers Equestrian Personality of the year.

2004 Highest place Brit at Athens Olympics on Escapado.

2005 I set up my own training yard in Gloucestershire.

relaxed but dancing for the entire test. In the Special we scored a personal best coming 3rd. It was quite emotional for me because it was my last ride on him but it was an incredible test, an incredible ride - one I will never forget.

My daily routine

I now have my own beautiful yard in Gloucestershire, England where I train horses, give lessons to clients and operate a small breeding operation. The design of the farm is based on efficiency, having taken inspiration from many riding establishments I have visited throughout the world. My daily routine is always interspersed with travels throughout the country attending competitions and giving clinics. Over the years I have managed to meet many of Britain's top vets, blacksmiths, equine dentists and feed specialists who ensure all of my horses remain in good health.

How my riding career began

I grew up on a small Channel Island called Sark. When I was very young I ran errands for my mother on a donkey and later I drove a horse and carriage for tourists. I always loved horses but it wasn't until I made the leap from the island to mainland England that I was able to find a job working with horses. Initially I evented but when I was 19, I won the Young Dressage National Championship on a skewbald mare called Jolly Dolly and dressage became my life. For me the biggest opportunity came when Dr Wilfried Bechtolsheimer asked me to join his stable. The thought of riding magnificent horses, living in my own cottage and being paid was an unbelievable dream - it was an experience that changed my life. In the three years I was with the 'Bs' I rode his horses at the World Championships, the European Championships and the Barcelona Olympics. I then set up my own yard with a business colleague before moving to my own premises in 2005.

Sometimes the competitions can be wearing but I find training horses and riders inspiring. I like horses which are sensitive, have good conformation and possess that 'look of eagles'. For many years when I first started out and could not afford the 'big movers' I realised you can make a good horse better if it has the right temperament but perhaps not the flashy movement. The best riders to teach are those that have endless enthusiasm to do better and are tireless in their drive to achieve.

My Competition Highlights

1985 British Young Rider National Champion.

1990 Team 5th World Equestrian Games Stockholm on Rubelit von Unkenruf.

1991 3rd Grand Prix 5th Kur CDI Schoten on Rubelit. 1st Intermediaire I Goodwood National Championships on Giorgione.

1992 4th GP CDI's Hertogenbosch, 3rd Grand Prix and Special CDI-W Goodwood, 5th Grand Prix Special CDI Wiesbaden, Team 7th Barcelona Olympics, 1st Grand Prix British National Championships on Giorgione.

1993 5th Grand Prix 3rd Special CDI Goodwood on Giorgione.

1995 1st Pas De Deux European Championships on Gershwin.

1997 2nd Grand Prix 3rd Kur CDI Hickstead, 1st Grand Prix British National Championships on Legal Democrat.

1998 1st Grand Prix and Kur British National Championships on Legal Democrat.

1999 1st Grand Prix and Special CDI Stubbing Court, 1st Grand Prix and Kur British National Championships on Legal Democrat.

2000 3rd Grand Prix at Sunshine Tour Spain, 7th Grand Prix 2nd Special CDIO Hickstead, Team 8th Sydney Olympics on Argentille Gullit.

2001 1st Grand Prix CDIO Hickstead on Donnersong.

2007 1st Grand Prix and Special Sunshine Tour Spain, 2nd Grand Prix Special CDIO Rotterdam on Lecantos, 4th Grand Prix Kur CDI-W Olympia UK on Dolendo.

2008 1st Grand Prix 5th Special at Sunshine Tour Spain on Dolendo, 3rd Grand Prix 1st Special Saumur on Liebling II.

2009 Silver Team medal at Windsor European Championships on Leibling II.

By nature I am a relaxed person so I don't really need holidays to unwind, although I do enjoy wine tasting tours. After a few days I am ready to get back to the farm and the horses. We spend so much time at shows I find that I do most of my socializing with other competitors. I like people around me before a competition and only concentrate on the test ahead when I am on the horse. I told myself years ago that feeling pressure was an unnecessary evil that I would not succumb to.

Anna van Olst

The Trainer

My Story

I was born March 25th 1962in Denmark. Although I am married to Dutchman Gertjan van Olst and we live in Holland I am still a Danish national. I have been a member of the Danish dressage team for over 16 years and I have trained and competed more than 15 horses up to Grand Prix level. I grew up with non-horsey parents and started my riding career jumping horses. I was given my first dressage horse when I was 22 and there was no turning back - I loved it. Four years later I rode in my first Olympic Games at Seoul when Anky van Grunsven was riding Prisco. I have since competed in a total of 4 Olympic games, 3 World Championships, 6 European Championships and I have been Danish National Champion twice.

Training Carl and Escapado

I met Carl in Stockholm in 1990 at the World Championships. This was his first big international competition riding for his country. We stayed in touch over the next few years casually discussing horses over glasses of wine. I could see very early on that Carl shared my love of horses. We have a very good partnership in that we can talk about the bad points of our horses as well as the good, something that is not very common amonst competitors as often you do not want anyone to know the bad things about your horse. Gradually we started training together. Carl would come over to our stallion station in Holland and stay for a week or so. We would ride all day and then discuss the horses over dinner in the evening. In a way the training sessions went on for 24 hours. It was very intense but we got a lot out of it. Carl used to say that when you go to some trainers they try to make the lesson a positive experience so you never really work on the problems - this was not so with us. Carl and I are very honest with each other - ours is a relationship based on trust. I train other students some of whom train with me in Holland but live at Carl's in the UK - there is no jealously between us.

Escapado never found any of the Grand Prix movements difficult - he was very intelligent. If he appeared difficult it was rather him thinking - do I really have to do this, is it really necessary that I learn to do all of this? He was not a big horse and was very compact so he could be very quick and powerful - he was such an athlete. I have memories when I was riding him of us flying across the arena out of control when I was trying to teach him the tempi changes but even so you could see that he was going to be a talented Grand Prix horse. At this time Carl was not so convinced because Escapado was taking his time learning the tempi changes and Carl thought at one point he may never learn them. I bet Carl his new mobile phone that I could teach Escapado one time tempi changes in a week. Carl agreed and I won the phone.

Escapado has a lot of thoroughbred blood in his veins which contributed to his preference to run away if he didn't like a situation. If Escapado got tense this could be seen mainly in the canter pirouettes as he would stiffen

Anna's Competition Highlights

1988 Member of Danish Olympic Team Seoul.

1992 Member of Danish Olympic Team Barcelona.

2000 Member of Danish Olympic Team Sydney.

2007 9th Grand Prix 10th Kur at CDI-W Frankfurt on Exquis Clearwater.

2008 Team Bronze medal Hong Kong Olympics, 9th Grand Prix 8th Kur CDI-W Mechelen, 10th Grand Prix 9th Kur at

CDI-W Stockholm, 6th Grand Prix 7th Kur at CDI-W Odense, 16th Grand Prix14th Special 12th Kur at CDIO Aachen, 5th Grand Prix and Special at CDI Wiesbaden on Exquis Clearwater, 13th Grand Prix 8th Special at CDI Aachen, 12th Grand Prix10th Kur at CDI Wiesbaden on Dexter.

2009 10th Grand Prix 6th Kur Bronze Team medaL Nations' Cup at CDIO Rotterdam on Exquis Clearwater, 8th Grand Prix and Kur at CDI-W 's Hertogenbosch, 5th Team Grand Prix 21st Individual 26th Grand Prix Special European Championships at Windsor UK on Exquis Clearwater.

his back and jump through from behind rather than reaching with the hind leg. Once he was relaxed he found everything so easy. The trick was to keep finding ways to keep him chilled. Carl often used his voice quietly when riding a test as communication was important to Escapado. Indoor arenas were also a nerve-wracking experience as the audience could be noisey and seated very close so we stuck to outdoor venues. Turning him out for long periods in his field every day also broke the tension. Escapado's tension problems were overcome one by one with a great deal of patience.

When competing, Carl would always ride Escapado early in the morning or at least many hours before his test so that he would only need to do the briefest of warm ups just before he was due in the arena. Sometimes Escapado could be 'hot' before his test and a long warm up would just make him hotter. We would use this time to relax him and then just before he entered the arena he would practise the passage. In my opinion Carl is one of the most talented riders - he rides with such lightness and feeling and if Escapado did get hot during the test Carl could cope with it.

I train with the Danish team coach Rudolph Zeilinger but if you say who is my real trainer I would have to say it is Carl. If he is training me he gets something out of it and I also ride better for training him.

Opposite Anna leaving the arena on Exquis Clearwater after completing the Grand Prix test at Windsor 2009
Above, left Anna and Exquis Clearwater competing in the World Cup Qualifier at the Globe in Stockholm
Above Anna and Carl taking a break at the European Championships held at Windsor. Anna's team came 5th and Carl riding for Great Britain won the Silver Team medal

Escapado
The Horse

I met Escapado, or 'Peanuts' as we called him, for the first time when Michel Assouline called to say he had a five year old that I might like. Escapado was beautiful and he moved beautifully. He had the best hind leg which coupled with his 'sitability' and power was a combination that are not often seen together in horses. Escapado is not a big horse but he has a personality as big as a house and to manage him, as I was to find out later, took up most of my day. He had so much energy and there wasn't a moment when I did not think about him or what we had to do with him or how many hours we had to have him out of his stable so he could burn off some of this energy. When he was out in his field he

Above *Escapado leaving the arena at Aachen after completing the Grand Prix where he came 2nd for his new owner Hans Peter Minderhoud*
Right *Carl and Escapado in piaffe at Hickstead*
Top *Escapado and his friend Dolendo relaxing in their field at Carl's*

Escapado's Competition Highlights

2002 1st British National Championships, Prix St. Georges and Intermediaire 1.

2003 1st Intermediaire II Grand Prix, Special and Kur at Sunshine Tour Spain, 2nd Grand Prix Special CDI Pegaso Italy, 1st Grand Prix Special CEI-W Lipica Slovenia, 2nd Grand Prix and Special CDI Saumur France, British Team Reserve for European Championships Hickstead.

2004 1st World Cup Qualifier Mechelen, 1st Grand Prix, Special and Kur at Sunshine Tour Spain, 1st CHIO Hickstead UK, Team 7th Athens Olympics, 1st Grand Prix and Kur British National Championships, 4th Grand Prix

Kur CDI-W Maastricht, 2nd Grand Prix and Kur CDI-W Olympia UK.

2005 5th GP CDI 's Hertogenbosch, 9th Grand Prix at World Cup Final Las Vegas, 1st Grand Prix and Kur CDI Hartpury UK, 7th Grand Prix 3rd Special European Championships.

2007 9th Grand Prix 3rd Special at CDIO Aachen with Hans Peter Minderhoud

2008 3rd Grand Prix 2nd Kur CDI Maastricht, 1st Grand Prix and Kur CDI Odense, 3rd Grand Prix 1st Kur CDI Flynge with Hans Peter Minderhoud.

2009 1st GP and Kur CDI Zwolle, 2nd Grand Prix 1st Kur CDI Aachen with Hans Peter Minderhoud.

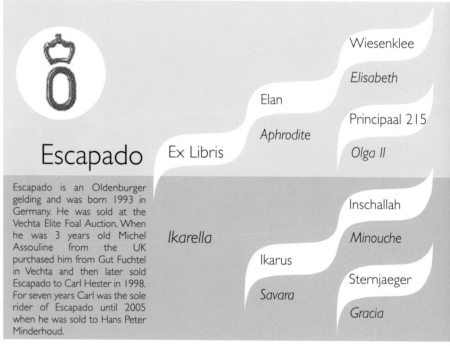

Escapado   Ex Libris — Elan — Wiesenklee / Elisabeth; Aphrodite — Principaal 215 / Olga II. Ikarella — Ikarus — Inschallah / Minouche; Savara — Sternjaeger / Gracia.

Escapado is an Oldenburger gelding and was born 1993 in Germany. He was sold at the Vechta Elite Foal Auction. When he was 3 years old Michel Assouline from the UK purchased him from Gut Fuchtel in Vechta and then later sold Escapado to Carl Hester in 1998. For seven years Carl was the sole rider of Escapado until 2005 when he was sold to Hans Peter Minderhoud.

would run and run whinnying to all the other horses. He was so clever that at times he was not the easiest horse to train. No one could take anything out of him that he did not want to give - he took care of himself. But he was a horse that could learn the wrong things just as easily as the good things. The grooms would hack him out most days and I would concentrate on his training which after many patient months and years started to produce results.

Escapado was never horrendous, he never bucked or reared. He had an immense willingness to please me all the time. He would not spook at things he saw but the flight mechanism, which horses possess, would trigger off every time he heard strange noises. Our training facility at the time was only 100 yards from a major road so he was always running off at the sounds of horns and air-brakes. There were times when I thought he would never settle. At shows he was so insecure that when he had to leave the other horses to do his test he would neigh continuously - even when doing the Grand Prix. His three lovely paces in the beginning were always affected by tension. But over time this tension was replaced by trust in the people who handled him and in his familiarity with his routine and environment.

At home he became the loveliest horse you could ever meet. Everyone who came to the stables loved him - he

would tilt his head so they could scratch his ears and he would become all cuddly.

When I sold Escapado to the Exquis group for Hans Peter Minderhoud to ride I intended to take a year off to recuperate, it was such a bittersweet split, his huge personality had made my life impossible but in six months I was chomping at the bit to get going again. Escapado is very happy at his new home and is doing so well in his competitive life. Anna has worked and competed with Hans Peter for many years so I know Peanuts is in very caring hands. He still recognizes me and his old groom Caroline who now works for Anna.

Carl Hester and Escapado

Competing in Prix St Georges at the 2002 CDN at Hickstead in the early of days of Escapado's competitive dressage career, already the expression and lightness in his movements is evident. Carl and Escapado went on to win this class and also the Intermediaire I.

Carl has been for many years and still is one of the most popular horsemen in England. His clinics are much sought after as the audience enjoy his mix of making riding fun with his technical ability to get the best out of each horse he rides. Carl is the complete professional, in that he rides and trains each horse in a way which suits their individual temperaments and athletism enabling him to maximize their ability. The level of care each horse receives in Carl's yard is tailored to their specific requirements and is second to none.

Harmony

Debbie McDonald and Brentina

The harmonious interaction between horse and rider can only be achieved when all of the criteria of the training scale have been established: rhythm, suppleness, contact, impulsion, straightness and finally collection. Harmony is demonstrated by the horse carrying out the wishes of the rider without the slightest resistance, and with a willing yet not subservient acceptance of the aids, thereby appearing to perform each of the movements of the test as if of his own accord.

To have witnessed the development of this amazing combination, having judged them from the lower levels of dressage in National competitions in the USA, right through to their glorious performances in international competitions, particularly at the World Equestrian Games in Jerez in 2002, has been one of the greatest privileges I can remember during my time as an FEI Judge. In fact, if my memory serves me correctly, I had them a mark or two ahead of everyone after the three competitions at the World Games in Jerez and personally would not have been unhappy if they had been crowned World Champions due to their beautifully consistent and harmonious performances.

Top dressage horses come in many guises and all have their strengths and weaknesses. Brentina might not have been the most power packed equine athlete with 'eyes on stalks' and 'breathing fire' but to see the trust in those big soft eyes and the contented expression on her face after completing a particularly good exercise certainly deserved recognition. The rapport between Debbie and Brentina has been an inspiration to so many up and coming riders, not only in the United States, but also Worldwide. This rapport was a reflection of the knowledgeable long term patient training Brentina had received from Debbie and also the complete trust they had in each other which had developed over the years.

It is quite amazing how few competitions this combination actually attended, which goes to show how important it is to conduct correct training at home. Debbie also did not 'convert' to dressage until relatively late in her equestrian career compared to many dressage riders. She first fulfiled a successful profession, training and competing hunters and jumpers and if it had not been due to the misfortune of a bad accident while jumping, the United States dressage world may never have had the privilege of this combination representing them at the Olympics, Pan American Games and several World Cup Finals. Debbie's deep understanding of her horses and in particular, Brentina, coupled with her experience and knowledge of how to train horses made the transition from jumpers to dressage a natural move for her and her team. As Debbie had pointed out herself, many times she didn't realise that she had been teaching her jumping horses dressage movements all along, without knowing it was called dressage.

Debbie's quiet unassuming style and the genuine and systematic training techniques that she has applied to the education of this generous mare, are, without doubt, something to be both applauded and celebrated. Debbie has been a great ambassador for the sport and although Brentina is now enjoying a very well deserved retirement, it would be great to see Debbie once again coming down the centre line on a new partner who has benefitted from such an understanding rider.

Above *A very pleased Debbie McDonald on Brentina having just completed their Grand Prix test at the 2002 World Equestrian Games in Jerez de la Frontera, Spain*
Opposite *Debbie's many expressions of happiness having just completed the Grand Prix test at the 2005 World Cup Final in Las Vegas where they placed third behind Edward Gal on Lingh and Anky Van Grunsven on Salinero*

Debbie McDonald

The Rider

My most memorable test

Brentina actually has not done many big Grand Prix tests in her life. In fact, people in Europe would be shocked at how few we have done. We go out only three to five times a year to major CDI tournaments, partly because there are not many big dressage competitions held in the US and also because where we live, in a rather secluded part of Idaho, makes it difficult to travel. It was at the Pan American Games in Winnipeg in 1999 where Brentina won the Individual Gold and Team Gold medals as a young nine year old that I first realised how much potential she had. But it was the World Cup Finals in Las Vegas in 2005 that counts as our most memorable test. It was an amazing experience, competing at such a big competition on home ground and in front of such a large audience seated in the Thomas & Mack arena. What made it even more special was that this arena was built by my long term sponsor and Brentina's owner Perry Thomas.

Before this competition I had become discouraged and felt I needed to change my approach to competitive dressage, so I decided just to have fun and create a new freestyle. I had chosen the song *Respect* by Arethra Franklin as I wanted to make a statement that I really didn't think my mare Brentina was receiving the respect she deserved. To use such modern soul music was new and something of a gamble - I really didn't know what the judges would think but I knew the audience would get into it - and they truly did. The crowd went wild clapping to the beat of the music. We got a standing ovation from over 8,000 members of the audience that day. It was just the most amazing feeling, one I shall never forget.

My Story

1954 I was born on 27th August in Pamona, California.

1966 Flannigan was my very first pony that my parents bought for me but I had to maintain him.

1988 My husband Bob McDonald encouraged me to take up dressage after a bad show jumping accident.

1994 I met three year old Brentina for the first time at the Elite Auction in Verden.

1999 I am named the Equestrian of the Year by the USEF and the Female Equestrian Athlete of the Year by the USOC.

2008 Brentina retires after taking part in her last major competition at the Olympics in Hong Kong

2009 I am awarded the USEF Developmental Coach of the year.

My daily routine

Work normally starts for me at 7:30am. I ride in the morning and teach in the afternoon, finishing around five o'clock. Now that I am not competing so much my routine has changed. I used to ride six or seven horses a day, but now that I have wonderful students I only need to ride three horses each day. My main focus is now on coaching young riders and particularly my protégé, Adrianne Lyle. I try to be to my students the sort of trainer that I appreciated having - a good trainer must be consistent and not change riding styles from one day to the next and not push the rider or the horse too fast. Most of all a good trainer must have a true love and passion for horses rather than it just being a job.

How my riding career began

I caught the 'horse bug' spending summers on my uncle's ranch in Kansas. When I was 12, I managed to persuade my parents to buy me a pony called Flannigan, promising that I would pay for the upkeep of the pony myself. I found a place to keep him at the local county fairground where there was also a trainer. He allowed me to work for my pony's board. When I was 14, I remember being horrified to find this trainer in my pony's stable, with a whip in his hand, abusively trying to teach Flannigan to stand up on his hind legs. At that point I went looking for a new stable which is when I met Bob McDonald, my future husband. Bob has great horsemanship skills and I had every faith in his training. He soon became my trainer and mentor, whilst I was riding hunters and jumpers. I worked as a groom for

him for nine years before we were eventually married.

My interest in dressage was not due to a desire to take up the sport, it was a result of having suffered a bad fall riding hunters and jumpers which had been my main passion since I started riding. Peggy Thomas, my long term sponsor, always had an interest in dressage and she suggested I try it. Bob also thought I should take it up and we soon realised that the way we had brought on our hunters and jumpers was in fact similar to the way basic dressage movements were taught, we only called it by different names. Hilda Gurney was my first dressage trainer who did all the initial lunge work with me. I have also had great help from Lilo Fore and from my peers and team mates, Steffen Peters and Gunter Seidel. It has not been easy to get help where we live, so most of the time I worked on my own. River Grove Farm is in a rather isolated location in Sun Valley, Idaho and to get here you have to take two airplanes and then a small light plane. Looking back, I was very fortunate indeed to have Klaus Balkenhol come to help me with Brentina so many times, as he had to come all the way from Germany.

My Competition Highlights

1999 1st individual and Team Gold Pan American Games.

2002 4th Individual, Team Silver World Equestrian Games Jerez Spain.

2003 1st Bayer Festival of Champions, 1st World Cup Championship Sweden, Silver Nations Cup CHIO Aachen.

2004 Team Bronze Athens Olympics. 1st US Grand Prix Freestyle Championships/US League Final.

2005 1st US Grand Prix Freestyle Championships/US League Final.

2006 Team Bronze World Equestrian Games Aachen.

2008 Team 4th Beijing Olympics.

Above *Klaus Balkenhol, the trainer of many successful International riders such as Debbie McDonald, Nadine Capellmann and Laura Bechtolsheimer. Klaus gained much of his experience from training and competing on his own horses. His most successful horse, Goldstern, was purchased for him as a promising police horse*

Opposite *The American Team at the award ceremony for the Nation Cup winners at the 2003 CDIO in Aachen in which they won the Silver medal behind the German Team. Team members included Steffen Peters on Grandeur, Lisa Wilcox (shown here with Debbie and the US Team Chef d'Equipe Klaus Balkenhol) and Günter Seidel on Nikolaus 7*

Klaus Balkenhol

The Trainer

Training Debbie and Brentina

I first met Debbie when she arranged to come to Warendorf in Germany to train with me. Brentina was just six years old at that time. Debbie did not speak German and I did not speak very good English, but when it came to training Brentina we didn't have any problems understanding each other at all. Debbie is such an accomplished rider with an exemplary feel of horses, she exudes enthusiasm and so together with her enormous support from the Thomas family it was very motivating to work with them. I also trained Debbie and Brentina in my official capacity as Team coach for the USA dressage team.

In training we focused a lot on the technical side of riding, but always in moderate doses so as not to overtax Brentina. Debbie had brought three other horses with her from America on this first occasion so she was kept very busy with all the training.

My first impressions of Brentina were that she had very good foundation paces, she was keen to work and did not have any vices. She had been brought on by Debbie very sympathetically and very correctly. Her walk was really good and she would get her highest marks in both the collected and extended walk. In the trot she would work through her body. Her canter was good but became much better through gymnastic training. As she matured in her training the collected paces became her speciality, such as the piaffe, passage along with the pirouettes. Because Brentina has such impulsion it made training her so easy. Mentally she was always ready to work.

Brentina really was Debbie's horse and she could be very 'tricky' when someone else tried to ride her. The partnership between them was unbelievable, you could almost say they were soul mates. Debbie loved that horse and Brentina knew it and gave so much of herself back to Debbie. Debbie was establishing this same relationship with her other three young horses as well. This was an indication of the type of person Debbie was, in that it mattered to her that her horses liked her and liked what they were doing.

It is quite remarkable how well Debbie and Brentina did on the International scene, considering that they did not have the same opportunities to compete compared to other horse and rider combinations in Europe as there are far fewer major competitions in the US. When you are able to compete more frequently, as they do in Europe, the horse and rider can establish a track that they follow. There are less surprises and the horses can be more settled. Yet Brentina was very good in that she worked exactly the same way at competitions as she did at home. Debbie had her own routine and method she used to prepare Brentina and she was always consistent with this. She would warm her up, spending quite some time in walk, really focusing on keeping Brentina relaxed so there was no tension anywhere in her body or in her head. Debbie really had an understanding of everything going on around her, and was always fair to her horse. Once she had Brentina really relaxed and supple, she would be ready for the more complicated movements.

Brentina is now enjoying a well deserved retirement and may even produce a foal. Debbie is focused more than ever on teaching talented, up and coming young riders. As for myself, I have no plans to give up my work training horses and riders just yet. Why would I want to give up something I enjoy and that keeps me so young!

Brentina

The Horse

A day in the life

Brentina is a 16'2" Hanoverian chestnut mare. I first saw her at the Elite Auction in Verden. We arrived five days before the auction and the thing that really struck me about her was the consistency she showed in her work, day after day, and she was only three years old. Both my husband and I value a horse with an attitude like this - we both believe it can make up for less brilliant paces. What a horse lacks in talent, if it has the right attitude and accepts the work, can be overcome with good consistent work. I have never had an argument with Brentina and she has never had a bad day. She is so confident and just loves to work.

  Brentina is now retired, but when she was in work, her typical day included going on the horse walker for 45 minutes in the morning, then she would go back to her stable for a couple of hours to relax and eat hay. Later I would ride her for 45 minutes. Not all of her riding time was spent schooling, as she did everything so well I didn't need to repeat things a lot. Most of the time it was just working on the basics, often perfecting the transitions that were in the Grand Prix test, rather than focusing on maintaining the movement for long periods. After our ride, Brentina would go out to her pasture for a couple of hours, before returning to her stable for

Above *Brentina and Debbie competing in the 2008 Beijing Olympics*
Right *Brentina at her retirement celebration along with her groom Ruben Palomera, Debbie, Debbie's husband Bob and Brentina's owners, Peggy, Jane and Parry Thomas*
Opposite, top *Brentina and Debbie ready to do their trot-up before the start of the dressage competition at the Beijing Olympics*
Opposite, bottom *Brentina showing off her ground covering extended trot at the Beijing Olympics. Brentina found the large media screens, which the horses could see from the arena while they were performing their tests, very distracting which prevented her from executing the test to her usual high standards*

1999 Team and Individual Gold at the Pan American Games.

2001 USET Grand Prix Champion.

2002 USET Grand Prix Champion, Team Silver, Individual 4th WEG Jerez Spain, 1st US Freestyle Champion.

2003 2nd Grand Prix and Kur at World Cup Final Champion in Goteborg Sweden - later proclaimed the winner, Silver Team medal and 3rd Individual Nations Cup at CDIO Aachen, 1st Bayer Festival of Champions.

2004 Team Bronze Athens Olympics; 1st CDI Grand Prix and GP Special Dortmund Germany, 1st US Freestyle Champion.

2005 3rd FEI World Cup Finals Las Vegas, 1st Grand Prix Kur U.S. League Finals.

2006 Team Bronze World Equestrian Games at Aachen 9th individually.

2008 Participated at Beijing Olympics, this was to be her final competition.

2009 Brentina retired from dressage competitions in a special ceremony at the Las Vegas World Cup Final.

another rest. Later in the afternoon, she would go back on the horse walker again for another 45 minutes.

At competitions I did not change her routine or the way we worked. The only real difference was that she could not go out to pasture and she had to be hand walked rather than going on her horse walker. Our riding routine stayed the same but I would ride through the test a few times, more to get it back into my mind than anything else.

Brentina is very confident and doesn't particularly like other horses. You can take her anywhere and she is always very comfortable just being on her own. She loves people and acts more like a pet. She has a lovely soft look in her eye and if you are patting her she is so content - loving every minute of it. If you go to walk away, she will pull you back to her chest with her nose, almost pulling you over. She doesn't really like being brushed or tacked up, she just likes to stand near you.

On the other hand Brentina can be funny to ride. She has never thrown me, but she can be tricky for other riders. I am only 5ft high, so if she feels the weight or leg length of a different rider, she immediately knows it is not her mum and can be very objectionable.

Brentina was purchased initially to be ridden by Mrs Thomas but she was unseated and so the ride was passed to me. From the first time I sat on her, it just felt right. I wouldn't say Brentina was the flashiest horse I have ever ridden. For me more isn't always better but in the classical sense her paces were correct and I prefer this to what we often see out there in the arena these days. I've ridden many horses in my time, but Brentina truly has been my horse of a lifetime.

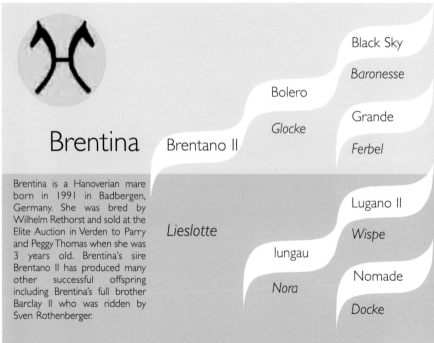

Brentina

Brentina is a Hanoverian mare born in 1991 in Badbergen, Germany. She was bred by Wilhelm Rethorst and sold at the Elite Auction in Verden to Parry and Peggy Thomas when she was 3 years old. Brentina's sire Brentano II has produced many other successful offspring including Brentina's full brother Barclay II who was ridden by Sven Rothenberger.

Brentano II	Bolero	Black Sky
		Baronesse
	Glocke	Grande
		Ferbel
Lieslotte	Iungau	Lugano II
		Wispe
	Nora	Nomade
		Docke

Brentina's Retirement Party

At the 2009 World Cup Finals in Las Vegas a special
ceremony was held for the well deserved retirement of
Mr. and Mrs Thomas' big chestnut mare Brentina. In
front of thousands of her adoring fans Brentina and
Debbie McDonald entered the dressage arena for the
last time. There was not a dry eye in the Thomas &
Mack centre as Brentina and Debbie made their way
into the centre of the arena to be met by the Thomas
family, Debbie's husband Bob, Brentina's long-time,
devoted, groom Ruben Palomera and other friends.

The Thomas & Mack Center
*The Thomas & Mack Center was built in 1983 and is located on the
campus of the University of Nevada Las Vegas in the United States.
Named after E Parry Thomas and Jerome Mack, both bankers from
Nevada, who donated funds for the feasibility and land studies. Much
happens in the Thomas & Mack Centre including rodeos, basketball,
wrestling, hockey and concerts*

BRENTINA

2006 WORLD EQUESTRIAN GAMES
2004 ATHENS OLYMPIC TEAM
2002 WORLD EQUESTRIAN GAMES
2001 U.S. NATIONAL CHAMPION
3-TIME U.S. FREESTYLE & LEAGUE FINAL CHAMPION
2-TIME U.S. DRESSAGE TEAM - CDIO AACHEN, GERMANY

AMERICA'S DRESSAGE HORSE

Halt and Salute

Kyra Kyrklund and Max

At the halt, the horse should be perfectly balanced with well engaged hindquarters. He should be attentive and straight whilst remaining completely immobile. The weight should be evenly distributed over all four legs, being by pairs abreast with each other. The neck should be raised and arched with the poll as the highest point and the front line of the face slightly in front of the vertical, while remaining 'on the bit' and maintaining a light and soft contact with the rider's hand. The horse may quietly chew the bit and should be ready to move off at the slightest indication of the rider.

Here we see the ultimate professional Kyra Kyrklund with her latest 'star' Max. In this picture we see Kyra and Max demonstrating the perfect halt and salute. Kyra's posture is, as usual, absolutely immaculate, with Max standing perfectly balanced, four square, fully attentive to his rider. His keen, alert expression showing clearly that he is ready to react instantly to his rider's next command. his straightness and beautiful carriage with his well engaged hind quarters and his gracefully arched neck, poll correctly the highest part, and showing a soft and acceptant contact with the bit is from the first movement of the competition more than enough to convince the Ground Jury and the public that this is a correctly trained athlete which is perfectly in tune with his rider.

It is sometimes easy to forget that the entry, halt and move off carry the same ten points as, for instance, a line of fifteen one time changes! Having had the privilege to witness Kyra's extraordinary and brilliant performances over quite a few years now, with so many horses, of course the most famous being the wonderful Matador, I have always found it fascinating to watch the systematic build up of her horses, both physically and mentally with each passing season. It is surely a testament to Kyra's superb riding and training that she can produce one horse after another to the highest level possible, with this rare ability to quietly allow each one of them to unlock its full potential until they are able to perform to the maximum and yet still appear completely natural and at peace with the world.

It is very exciting to think that both Kyra and her husband, Richard White, are now able to pass this wholesome attitude on to future generations of riders. Not only does Kyra compete at the highest level of dressage with Richard always present as her trainer but they also train many other competitors who compete against them. Kyra's teaching opinions are hotly sought after and she often shares her views at dressage clinics, conferences and national conventions. Kyra has also found the time to systemize her training techniques in her own published works.

To cope with your own pressure and demands that any competition will place on you is one thing but to also prepare other competitors at the same competitions would appear to be unbearable pressure for most people but Kyra always seems not phased by the stress and pressure and remains totally focused on the tasks at hand. Her professional attitude takes her from top rider status one minute to top coach and teacher the next and she is very successful at both. Kyra's students include many top team members who represent their countries at the highest level of dressage which includes the Olympics, The Europeans and World Cup Finals.

Showing absolutely no sign of slowing down her competitive career we look forward to many more excellent performances by Kyra and Max. Who knows perhaps Kyra has a few more rising stars waiting in the wings to be developed.

Kyra Kyrklund

The Rider

My most memorable test

Over the years I have competed in some of the biggest and busiest venues. To cope with competition pressure I have developed the technique, as many riders have, of simply blocking out everything beyond the dressage arena until the final halt and salute then I allow myself to look around. I have followed this routine religiously show after show until the 2006 World Equestrian Game in Aachen. The organisers of this event promised it would be a big one but I had no idea the Grand Prix Kur would be so well attended with close to 60,000 people filling the stadium. To Max, the more people that come to see him the better as he always does his best when the stadiums are full. For me it was totally unbelievable that so many people came to watch dressage. The atmosphere was amazing and electric. I had planned in my mind before the test that I would allow myself, just this once, to break my concentration and to look up at the crowds during the extended walk across the arena - to memorise the moment. What I saw will stay with me forever. Never in my wildest dreams did I think that dressage would become so big to take on a football match feeling it was such an achievement for dressage. To ride the test in an atmosphere like that was truly amazing.

My daily routine

My career with horses has grown over many years and today my schedule is not so much taken up with daily riding but with clinics, demonstrations, writing books, international competitions, student training and television programmes, all of which can take me anywhere in the world. The

Above *Max and Kyra on their victory lap at the 2008 World Cup Final in 's Hertogenbosch*
Opposite, top *Sitting in the tack room at Snowhill Farm in England. Close to forty years accumulation of ribbons trophies and plaques adorn the walls*

My Story

1951 Born in Helsinki, my love of horses started early and I would ride my godmother's draught horses in the holidays.

1969 On my first horse, Kasper, we won the Finnish Junior Championships in dressage placed 2nd in eventing and 4th in jumping.

1972 I gave up plans to become a veterinarian to spend two years at Stromsholm, Sweden, learning the theoretical framework of riding. After a few years in Germany I returned to Finland to set up my own 'Helsinki Competition Stable' where I taught riding using elements from both the German and Swedish systems.

1991 Became Chief Dressage Trainer at Flyinge Stud in Sweden, and transformed it into an international centre for dressage.

1998 After seven years at Flyinge Richard and I set up our new riding base in England.

My Competition Highlights

1972 1st, Finnish Championships on Dragon.

1976 1st, Finnish Championships.

1977 1st, Finnish Championships.

1978 1st, Finnish Championships.

1979 1st, Finnish Championships. 1st, Scandinavian Championships on Piccolo.

1980 5th Moscow Olympics on Piccolo.

1983 1st, Finnish Championships.

1986 1st, Finnish Championships.

1987 1st, Finnish Championships. 7th, European Championships on Matador.

1988 1st, Finnish Championships. 6th Team and Individual 5th, Seoul Olympics on Matador.

1989 1st, Finnish Championships on Matador.

1990 Silver medal, World Equestrian Games in Stockholm on Matador.

1991 Gold, World Cup Finals, in Paris on Matador.

1992 5th Barcelona Olympics on Edinburg.

1993 4th European Championships in Lipica on Edinburg.

1994 4th, World Equestrian Games in the Hague. 3rd, World Cup Finals in Gothenburg on Edinburg.

1996 28th Grand Prix at Atlanta Olympics on Flyinge Amiral.

1997 9th, European Championships in Verden. 5th, World Cup Final in s'Hertogenbosch on Flyinge Amiral.

1998 9th World Equestrian Games in Rome on Flyinge Amiral, 6th World Cup Finals in Gothenburg on Master.

1999 8th Grand Prix 5th Special on Palladium at CDI Hickstead

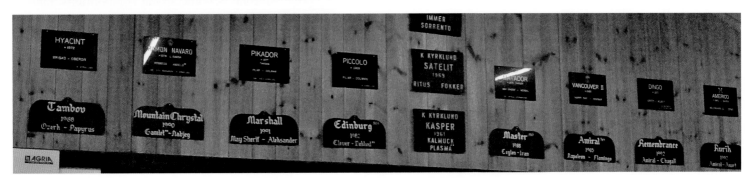

consistency in training required for Max and my other up and coming horses has to be planned thoroughly and strategically so that whatever my other commitments the horses get all that they need from me. Of course, to achieve this successfully takes the dedication and patience of a great team which I have.

How my riding career began

I can't remember when horses were not the centre of my life. My family did not own horses except for my godmother's draught horses. It was not until I was eighteen that I finally owned a horse of my own. Until then I borrowed, loaned and leased school horses so I could ride and compete. My passion and drive to learn all that I could about horses and riding was fuelled even more by the amazing training I have had, first from Walter Christensen in the 1970s and then from Herbert Rehbein in 1980 until his death in 1997. My own experiences and philosophy about the horse coupled with their training has enabled me to produce and compete fourteen different horses up to International Grand Prix level. I still feel there is so much more for me to learn about these wonderful animals.

Max and I have been training together for ten years and although he is still quite young for a Grand Prix horse I thought it was best to retire him from international competitions while the going was good. He is so honest, so willing and so consistent - he has achieved greater heights that anyone expected of him. Max is now going to help me on my lecture tours and clinics.

Richard White

The Trainer

Training Kyra and Max

Having known Kyra for over 18 years as her partner, trainer and now husband I have great respect for her concerns and talent when dealing with horses. She is one of the most experienced top riders in the world which makes training her a bit problematic for me as I am in awe of her capability of feeling and her depth of experience within the International Dressage world. But training together does work for us as Kyra is very open to try different things. She is not the sort of person who would take kindly to someone telling her 'you must ride like this or like that' or to keep repeating practices that do not work. Rather, we work together to find ways that work best for each horse. I am her eyes on the ground and as we share the same philosophy in training so we are usually working in the same direction. I ride at least six horses a day, including all of Kyra's, so I know a bit more about how her horses move and think, which is also helpful when Kyra is away and I pick up the training while she is gone, it maintains a continuity in the horses' progression.

Both Kyra and I have an extensive list of Grand Prix riders that we train at home and at competitions many of whom Kyra also competes against. Because I have also worked with all of her students I can step in and take over their warm-up when schedules are tight and Kyra has to be in the arena. This takes the pressure off Kyra and gives her time to prepare herself and Max for

the test ahead as she will often take herself away to a quiet corner where she can just concentrate on Max. Being organised is imperative for our business and we spend hours making lists of duties and routines before shows, during shows and after shows. Fortunately our students are encouraged to be independent so at shows there is not the problem of telling them what to do but rather watching to see if they have achieved the right feel or rhythm before they enter the arena. We don't use the shows for training, that happens at home, at shows we want to see if the students can achieve what they do at home. The best situation of course is one trainer to one rider, but it isn't like that in real life, at least not in ours. At Aachen one year we had 10 students and 8 students in Hong Kong at the Olympics. At one point I was wearing three headset microphones during the warm-up . . . it was the supreme test that our systems were working. . . and they did.

The best horse and rider combinations are those where the rider's ability and the horse's talent match. Riding

has to be a nice experience for both horse and rider and it is also a lot of hard work, so we try to match a horse with the ambitions and talent of the rider. You can tell a lot about a horses ability by its conformation. The rider must have 100% trust in me to work and co-operate with me. My training does not involve dominating the rider. The rider must be open-minded and willing to try new things if the training is to work. At the end of the day it is the rider's responsibility for how they ride.

Opposite *Richard White, Kyra's long term trainer and husband*
Opposite, bottom *Richard in Rotterdam coaching another famous student, Emma Hindle on Lancet*
Top *Kyra, Richard and the press at The European Championships at Windsor 2009*
Bottom, left *Richard debriefing a student at ringside after just completing their Grand Prix test*
Bottom, right *Richard, Kyra and Max's other owner Yvette Conn discussing strategies at Stuttgart*

Max
The Horse

A day in the life

I bought Max sight unseen in 1999. A phone call from a friend, who knows the sort of horses I like, said he was perfect 'had my name all over him' and was going to be sold at auction soon. What made him very special for me was that he was the son of Master, the horse I had ridden in the World Cup Final in 1998. When I bought Max and finally went to see him in Sweden I was a bit disappointed as his head and tummy appeared very large. But when I rode him I could feel there was a lot of talent there. I brought Max home to England but as Master was returning to Sweden the next night I had no stable for Max so he had to stay with my good friend Yvette Conn who lived next door. Yvette fell in love with Max from the start and insisted she become part owner of Max - not to ride him herself but to be part of the experience of watching a young horse go through the ranks to become a successful Grand Prix horse as she too had been charmed by Max and could see his talent.

Max is quite a calm horse now but he was more of a problem child when we first bought him, in fact one of the reasons he was sold at auction was due to him kicking several people. Something had gone wrong in his early life which left him frightened and insecure. Max was never a bad horse, he could become anxious in certain situations but over time he turned into a real

Above *Max and Kyra pleased with their test at the European Championships 2009*
Left *A few of the many stables at Kyra and Richard's charming Snowhill Farm in Surrey*

Max's Competition Highlights

2004 2nd Grand Prix, 1st Grand Prix Kur at CDIO, Hickstead.

2005 12th European Championships Hagen, Germany.

2006 12th Grand Prix Special, 7th, Grand Prix Kur, World Equestrian Games, Aachen.

2007 4th World Cup Final, Las Vegas, 4th Grand Prix, 2nd Grand Prix Kur World Cup Qualifier, Olympia, London.

2008 3rd World Cup Final at 's Hertogenbosch, 5th Grand Prix, 5th Grand Prix Special, 4th Grand Prix Kur at Aachen CHIO, 10th Grand Prix Special, 8th Grand Prix Kur at Bejing Olympics, 3rd Grand Prix and Kur at CDI-W London, 4th Grand Prix, 2nd Kur at CDI Stuttgart.

2009 1st Grand Prix and Kur CDI Addington, 5th Grand Prix 6th Kur CDI-W 's Hertogenbosch, 14th Grand Prix 9th Grand Prix Special 7th Grand Prix Kur at European Championships at Windsor Great Britain, Max retires from competition.

personality. A big turning point in Max's life was when he was about five and he had learned to do piaffe and passage. He suddenly started to trust people and would follow me everywhere. Now when he becomes nervous or anxious he will focus on people more than the scary situation that is going on around him. He has grown into a sugar loving super personality. At the end of every Grand Prix test Max expects to be given a sugar for being a good boy and he always gets one right after the final halt and salute.

I have been competing for many years on many different horses and in today's highly charged competitive world, the concerns of the horse are paramount in terms of his physical and mental well being. Care such as better arena surfaces, saddle fitters, dentists, physios, vets, blacksmiths - instead of waiting for a horse to go lame they are now looked after like athletes with a supportive team in place to monitor their every move. The competition horse is in a better environment today than he ever was.

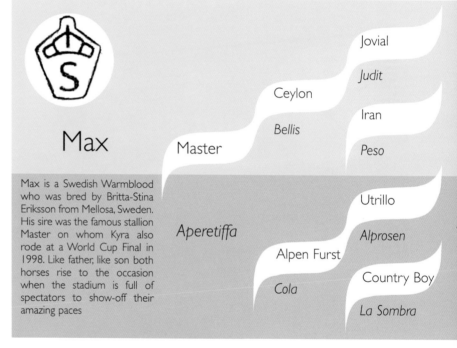

Max is a Swedish Warmblood who was bred by Britta-Stina Eriksson from Mellosa, Sweden. His sire was the famous stallion Master on whom Kyra also rode at a World Cup Final in 1998. Like father, like son both horses rise to the occasion when the stadium is full of spectators to show-off their amazing paces

Max

Master
— Ceylon
—— Jovial
—— Judit
— Bellis
—— Iran
—— Peso

Aperetiffa
— Alpen Furst
—— Utrillo
—— Alprosen
— Cola
—— Country Boy
—— La Sombra

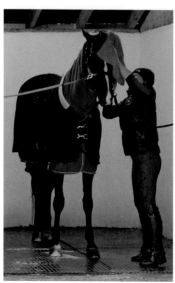

Above *Max showing off his expressive collected trot in front of the judges at the 2008 CDIO at Aachen*
Bottom *Max having a shampoo and bodywash in preparation for his next competition at London Olympia*

The Final Salute

Kyra and Max salute the judges after completing their Grand Prix test in the beautiful Aachen arena. There is always that moment of complete silence in the arena as horse and rider take their final salute before the crowd erupts with their appreciative applause.

There have been many changes in dressage throughout Kyra's long career and these beautiful venues that she now competes in, such as the CHIO at Aachen, are the result of endless hours put in by the event organizers and over 900 volunteers.

The CHIO at Aachen, how it all started
The inhabitants of Aachen in 1898 could not have imagined the horse races they staged in an attempt to liven up their day to day life would grow into the horse mecca that it is today. Over the past one hundred and eleven years many changes and additions were made to the site. Now over 800 of the World's best equestrians in Vaulting, Jumping, Driving, Dressage and Eventing congregate in the Soers each summer and over a period of 10 days compete for the much coveted prizes. Aachen's excellent facilities and management has made it popular as a venue for the European Championships, the World Equestrian Games and countless Olympic selection trials

Extended Walk

Edward Gal and Moorlands Totilas

The extended walk should cover as much ground forwards as possible, with the hind feet clearly overtracking the prints made by the front feet, whilst remaining in a perfectly regular four beat rhythm. The horse should appear relaxed with the energy flowing through the whole body, he should be marching forwards with eager, yet unhurried strides. The frame is allowed to lengthen as much as possible, while the elastic contact with the bit is maintained.

It may be somewhat surprising that we are showing Totilas, the Dressage phenomenon of the century, in one of the quietest exercises of the Grand Prix test, the Extended Walk! But. . . it is all the more extraordinary and impressive that this 'Mega' horse is able to come from his supercharged passage, that makes the hair on the back of the neck of the onlooker stand-up, to this totally relaxed and true extended walk.

I always think of the walk as being the 'tell-tale' exercise of every dressage test as it is impossible to disguise any weakness or faults in the training during the walk tour. If there is a contact problem that may not be obvious in the other exercises, more often than not, it will manifest itself during the walk by the horse taking the opportunity to drop the bit and draw back from the contact point.

If there is tension or anxiety that might be disguised as expression during the more impulsive movements, again usually there will be a problem in establishing a secure rhythm with enough relaxation and ground cover in the extended walk. As we can see this is certainly not the case with Totilas.

If there is actual physical stiffness in the horse's back, again there will be a problem during the walk which the horse may then be unable to develop a true four beat rhythm, or the steps may not be able to 'swing' through enough to show sufficient overtrack. This is not remotely evident in this illustration.

What is evident in this shot of Edward Gal and Totilas in the extended walk immediately following the passage, is that it is clear to see the picture of relaxation with the horse drawing forwards to an elastic and secure contact showing a correct lengthening of the frame with the front line of the face ahead of the vertical. Totilas is in a clear and regular four-time beat covering the ground and moving forwards, as if on his way home after a relaxing hack. Impressive indeed!

There are not enough complimentary words to say about this combination and the effect their talent and persona has had on the sporting scene this year. Edward's deep understanding of this young stallion and the trust Totilas has in Edward has made a fairytale storybook a reality. Never has dressage had a superstar burst onto the scene quite in the same way that Edward and Totilas have. The number of 10's awarded to them grows as Totilas becomes stronger and more confident, as do the number of World Records they are breaking for the Grand Prix, the Special and the Kur. What makes it so unbelievable is that this is his first season in Grand Prix and he is only nine years old.

Edward has as his support two trainers who are also his good friends who understand him and Totilas completely. Totilas' owners appreciate and value the athletic talent of their extraordinary young stallion over and above what must be the temptation to enter into a very promising breeding career. To watch a horse like Totilas perform is an unmissable opportunity, to ride a horse like Totilas must be a dream.

Edward Gal

The Rider

My most memorable test

For such a young horse, Totilas has accomplished so much. It was at the Dutch Nationals this year in the Grand Prix Special that I realised what an effect his performance was having on other people. We started our usual warm up, in which his first trot is more of a pony trot, and then after a few minutes I asked him for his bigger trot. He was as he has always been so mentally calm and consistent. I never have to put pressure on him and when I ask him for something, it is always there. When it was time to put him in competition frame, he began to really move and I felt that there was no end to what he was capable of giving me. This was our first Grand Prix Special, we had only done six Grand Prix tests before this. As our test got under way, Totilas had so much power and energy, I felt as if a bomb was going to go off but he never explodes which is good, and I kept saying to myself as he went from movement to movement - 'wow'. From trot to passage you only need to take him back a little and the same from passage to piaffe - he makes the advanced movements so easy, he just feels so good.

It was not until the final salute that I realised the audience was also moved. There were many spectators who were in tears - so inspired by Totilas' performance. When Totilas and I fit together so well it is emotional for me too and I do feel like crying. I have never ridden a horse like Totilas before. You think he is special because he is yours, but when other people are affected the same way you know he is very, very special. Totilas is so young and to think that as he grows stronger and more confident he will be better.

Above *Edward Gal leaving the arena in Rotterdam after completing another amazing performance on his black stallion, Totilas*
Opposite *Edward Gal on Totilas waving to a very appreciative audience at the CDIO Rotterdam, having just won the Grand Prix*

My Story

1970 I was born in Holland.

1984 I started riding an hour each week at a local riding stable. Soon people were asking me to ride their horses.

1993 Much to my Mother's horror I decided to take up riding as a full time profession.

1994 Nicole Werner and I set up our own yard and still train horses together today.

2006 Totilas came to our stable for training in preparation for the six year old championships.

2009 Totilas took the dressage world by storm winning the Dutch Nationals, the CDIO at Rotterdam, the World Dressage Masters at Hickstead and the European Championships at Windsor establishing new World Records along the way. There is still so much more to come.

How my riding career began

My riding career started quite late in comparison to many other riders. I was 14 before I rode regularly and that was only for one hour each week. Soon after people began to ask me to ride their horses if they were on holiday and it gradually built up from there. When I was 23 years old, I really was into horses and had to make the decision to continue with horses or to continue my education in economics. If I continued with my graduate work it meant travelling to other countries to work on projects leaving me with very little time to ride. To my Mother's horror, I chose riding. I lost my Father when I was only seven and my Mother was fearful that I would only be a stable hand and not be able to earn a proper living from horses, so I promised her if the horses did not work out I would resume my education when I was 25. Fortunately the horses just got better and better. I was lucky to get good horses to ride as many people were now asking me to train and compete their horses.

When I was looking for a place to keep my horses, I met Nicole Werner who already had stables and together we started up our own yard. Nicole has ridden to Grand Prix level and was very experienced but she now manages our very busy stables and has little time left to ride. My long term partner, Hans Peter Minderhoud also has about 15 horses at the same yard. Together Nicole and Hans Peter are my trainers. I generally ride eight or nine horses from 8am to 3pm and then spend the remainder of the day training students until 7pm. The days are always long but I never feel exhausted because I love it. If I really want to relax I cut the grass.

I feel it is the right time in my career to have a horse like Totilas. Perhaps if he had been my first Grand Prix horse I would not have been experienced enough to take him so slowly and may have found it too tempting and asked too much from him because he found it all so easy. With his talent I may have wanted to take him out more often to shows to show everyone how wonderful he was. To ride Totilas at the London Olympics is something I would really like to do. I just missed out going to the Athens Olympics with Lingh in 2004, as he had injured himself just before we were to go. However, the London Olympics are still a few years away, so for now I just want to enjoy every ride on him and perhaps if we are lucky we can fulfil our Olympic dream.

My Competition Highlights

2003 8th Grand Prix and Kur at CDI-W Maastricht on Lingh, 2nd Promising Stallions Finals at CDI Zwolle International Stallion Show on Gribaldi.

2004 1st Grand Prix, Special and Kur at Dutch Dressage Championships, 5th Grand Prix, Special and Kur at CDIO Aachen, 2nd Grand Prix and Kur at CDI-W 's Hertogenbosch, 3rd Grand Prix and 4th Kur at CDI-W Amsterdam on Lingh, 1st 6 yr old finals on Magic Rodrigo, 2nd Best Stallion on Gribaldi at CDI Zwolle International Stallion Show.

2005 2nd Grand Prix, 2nd Kur at CDI-W Maastricht, 1st Grand Prix, 2nd Special and Kur at Dutch Championships, 3rd Grand Prix, 2nd Kur at CDI-W 's Hertogenbosch, 1st Grand Prix and Kur at CDI-W Amsterdam on Lingh.

2006 3rd Grand Prix, 1st Kur at CDIO Rotterdam, 2nd Grand Prix, 1st Kur on Lingh, 2nd Grand Prix Special on Gribaldi at CDI Gelderland De Steeg, 6th Grand Prix, 4th Kur at CDI-W Finals Amsterdam, 2nd Grand Prix, 2nd Kur at CDI-W 's Hertogenbosch on Lingh.

2007 6th Grand Prix, 5th Kur at CDI-W at 's Hertogenbosch, 2nd Grand Prix, 3rd Kur at CDI-W Amsterdam on Gribaldi, 1st 6 yr old Young Stallion Final on United, 1st Best Stallion Grand Prix on Gribaldi at Zwolle International Stallion Show, 7th Grand Prix, 11th Kur at World Cup Final Las Vegas.

2008 1st Grand Prix, 2nd Special at CDI Flyinge, 2nd Grand Prix at CDI Maastricht, 1st Grand Prix, 1st Special at CDIO Rotterdam on Sisther de Jeu. 3rd Grand Prix Kur at CDI Cannes on Next One, 1st Grand Prix at CDN Zwolle on Next One.

2009 2nd Grand Prix CDIO Rotterdam on Sisther de Jeu, 7th Grand Prix CDI Zwolle on Next One.

Nicole Werner & Hans Peter Minderhoud

The Trainers

Training Edward and Totilas

It is unusual that a rider will have two trainers but Hans Peter, who is a very successful Grand Prix rider for the Netherlands, and I work together as Edward's trainers. We all get on very well, our outlook on training and horses is similar in some respects and different in others, which is good in that we have several approaches to training that we can adjust. Edward, Hans Peter and myself all work from the same premises which allows Hans Peter and Edward to ride together every day, sometimes changing horses so they can both feel how the horse is going before offering their opinions. I am the eyes on the ground or the talking mirrors as Peter calls me. If there is a big competition coming up we will take an hour out to watch the most important horse Edward or Hans Peter is taking. Despite Edward having two trainers we all realise that to be the best you cannot become totally dependent on your trainer you do not want to become a robot. We are passionate about the horses and so training is often done by negotiation.

We didn't think that Totilas' career would take off like this. Initially we thought he was quite expensive for a 5 year old that did not know his changes. When we tried him for the first time we brought a rider who rides young horses from our stables. He felt such power under him but had to kick him a little to get him to move. Totilas suddenly shot off round the arena out of control, our jaws dropped as we didn't know how to stop him. After the fourth lap Edward got on and has been his only rider since. The owners asked us to take him

Above *Hans Peter Minderhoud and Nicole Werner, Edward's trainers, taking a break at Hickstead*
Opposite, top *Hans Peter and Edward at Aachen. When Hans Peter, an exceptional Grand Prix rider, is competing Edward is there to lend his support and expertise*
Opposite, middle *Hans Peter, Nicole and Totilas' groom doing last minute preparations before Edward and Totilas enter the arena at The European Championships at Windsor. Edward and Totilas established World Records in the Grand Prix and Grand Prix Kur at Windsor*
Opposite, bottom *Edward and Totilas warming up in extended trot at Rotterdam*

Hans Peter's Competition Highlights

2004 4th 6 yr old finals at CDI Zwolle International Stallion Show on Rhodium.

2005 1st Third Level Final on Rhodium, 3rd Future Stallion on IPS Tango at Zwolle International Stallion Show.

2006 1st Future Stallion 5 yr old Final on Uptown, 1st 6 yr old Young Stallion on Florencio at Zwolle International Stallion Show.

2007 1st 6 yr old finals on Ucelli T at Zwolle International Stallion Show.

2008 5th Grand Prix, 2nd Kur on Nadine at CDI-W Olympia, 3rd Grand Prix, 2nd Kur on Escapado at CDI Maastricht, 9th Grand Prix, 7th Kur on Escapado at CDI-W Sweden, 11th Grand Prix, 7th Special, 5th Kur, Team Silver on Nadine at Hong Kong Olympics, 5th Grand Prix, 4th Special on Exquis Nadine at CDI-W 's Hertogenbosch.

2009 2nd Prix St Georges on Florencio, 2nd Grand Prix, 3rd Special, Team Gold medal on Exquis Nadine, 2nd CDI Grand Prix, 1st Kur on Exquis Escapado at CDIO Aachen, 1st Prix St Georges on Ucelli T, 2nd Prix St Georges on Florencio, 4th Grand Prix, Special and Kur on Nadine at Dutch Championships, 2nd Prix St Georges on Florencio at CDIO Rotterdam, 1st Prix St Georges on Tango, 1st Grand Prix and Kur on Escapado at CDI Zwolle, 4th Grand Prix and Kur on Exquis Nadine at Las Vegas Cup Final.

home and prepare him for the 6 year old Young Horse World Championships. It took about four or five months to teach him everything he needed to know for this competition, after that we called our sponsors to come and look at Totilas again - we could now see the magic. This horse and Edward were born for each other - the harmony between them is just incredible.

The three of us have had many trainers but all three of us have trained with Anky and Sjef and we have found that selective elements of their system work best for Totilas. Anky and Sjef have also taught us to be very professional in our approach to training and working towards a competition. But teaching Totilas is easy as he is very, very intelligent, full of energy, has a natural talent for everything and never argues.

Totilas

The Horse

A day in the life

I had first seen Totilas, or 'Toto' as we call him at home, competing in the 5 year old classes at the World Championships and I liked him instantly. Shortly after, we heard he was for sale so we went with our sponsors to look at him. The first time I rode him I didn't know what to think, I liked his movement but there was so much power that you were almost afraid - can I control this? - is it too much? The owners allowed me to take Totilas home to my stables for a month and here we really developed a connection.

When Toto is at home he is so chilled. He loves to be with people and when people are around he comes to his door to be patted. Despite being a stallion he is very still and does not bite, he is like a shy innocent little boy. The only thing with him is that sometimes he is not very brave. When in the washing stall there is a small drain on the floor and he finds this ever so scary. He has been there for three years but he is still frightened of it. Everyday he is hand walked out in his field. When we first got him we turned him out and he just went mad, we thought he would break his legs. Now he is allowed to buck and kick on the lunge line where we still have a little control. I always think with him that if he gets totally out of control, I may never get him back again. This is how I felt the first time I sat on him.

Toto is not used for breeding at the moment. The owners are very focused on a competition career for him and then perhaps later concentrate on breeding. I think he would be a different horse if he was used for breeding and maybe not do so well in the arena.

I have never had this connection with a horse before. We don't practice the halt or standing still - when I relax, he relaxes and when I pick up, he picks up. He has this extraordinary ability to interpret my subtle moves and I know that he has total trust in me. I have never felt a horse like this and he can learn so quickly and make it look so easy - it is not normal. Already he can do everything at home for 10's. He doesn't always succeed in the ring but as he matures he will. At the

Above *Moorlands Totilas leaving the arena at Hickstead*
Right *The score board at Hickstead showing the new World Record achieved by Edward and Totilas in the Grand Prix Kur. At the Europeans at Windsor at few weeks later Edward and Totilas smashed this record with a score of 90.75%*
Opposite, top *Edward and Totilas at the 'Trot up' at Hickstead. All horses and ponies competing at International competitions must first be inspected by a team of veterinarians to ensure they are sound and in good health before they compete*
Opposite, left and right *Edward and Totilas executing extended canter and canter pirouette at the CDIO at Rotterdam 2009*

Totilas' Competition Highlights

Stallion Show in the Netherlands.

2007 1st Prix St Georges at Schaijk.

2008 1st Prix St Georges CDI Flyinge, 1st Prix St Georges and Intermediaire I Kur at CDI Rotterdam, 1st Intermediaire I and Kur at CDI-W Amsterdam, 1st Prix St Georges and 1st Intermediaire I Kur Promising Stallion at Zwolle International

2009 1st Grand Prix, Special and Kur Dutch Championships, 1st Grand Prix and Kur at CDIO Rotterdam, 1st World Dressage Masters Grand Prix and Kur (World Record) at CDIO Hickstead UK, Team Gold medal (World Record) Silver medal Grand Prix Special Gold medal Grand Prix Kur (World Record) at European Championships Windsor UK.

Dutch Nationals he received many, many 10's but always for different things - it is so encouraging.

Toto is still such a young horse. Sometimes when we return from a competition, I can see that he is very strong in his body but his mind is tired, so we give him time to be quiet and then bring him on slowly again. For the moment there is little pressure on him and his competition life is fun. I know in the arena he can be much better than this but if I became too eager then perhaps it would not be so much fun for him. He doesn't need to be doing anything differently at the moment, he has beaten everyone.

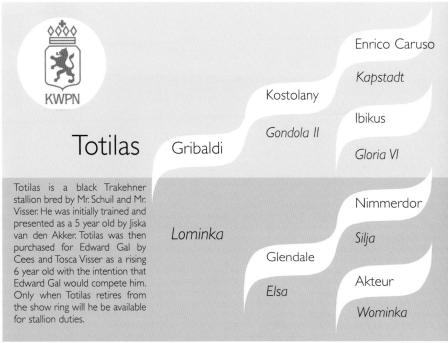

KWPN

Totilas

Totilas is a black Trakehner stallion bred by Mr. Schuil and Mr. Visser. He was initially trained and presented as a 5 year old by Jiska van den Akker. Totilas was then purchased for Edward Gal by Cees and Tosca Visser as a rising 6 year old with the intention that Edward Gal would compete him. Only when Totilas retires from the show ring will he be available for stallion duties.

			Enrico Caruso
		Kostolany	*Kapstadt*
Gribaldi			Ibikus
		Gondola II	*Gloria VI*
Lominka			Nimmerdor
		Glendale	*Silja*
		Elsa	Akteur
			Wominka

Edward Gal, Totilas and Friends

The Grand Prix Kur has brought dressage into the forefront of 'must see' sporting events. Beautiful horses, creative floor routines set to bespoke music has attracted the attention of many spectators who might otherwise not have attended a dressage event. If you are lucky to secure V.I.P. hospitality, which is much in demand at CDIO venues, and witness the creation of a new World Record, you have a memory that should last a lifetime.

Edward Gal on Moorland's Totilas stunned the audience at Hickstead by producing the best ever Grand Prix Kur. A few weeks later at The Europeans held at Windsor, Totilas set a new World Record for the Grand Prix and Kur. Totilas is only nine years old, quite young for a Grand Prix horse, let alone setting World Records, and he still has lots to learn. One can only expect that with more experience and fewer mistakes made during the performance, his marks should rise even higher. Edward who has a deep understanding of how to bring the best out in the black stallion has been very patient with Totilas' training and competitive career.

Dressage at Hickstead

Dressage at Hickstead was established in 1993 by Dane Rawlins, an international rider for Great Britain and trainer to many Grand Prix riders. Identifying the need for a top rate show facility in the South of England, Dane and his supporters have created what is undoubtedly one of the best dressage facilities in the UK. The venue has grown over the years in both popularity and the facilities it can offer to horses, riders and spectators. Recognising that not all riders compete at the highest levels of dressage, many competitions are held at Hickstead throughout the year for British 'unaffiliated' dressage riders. Also, youth camps for children with their ponies and horses are organised during the summer here.

Dressage at Hickstead offers one of the best facilities in Britain and is now considered to be a world-class show venue. In 2003, Dressage at Hickstead hosted the European Dressage Championships and each year a CDIO is held at Hickstead attracting riders from all over the world.

Collected Trot

Isabell Werth and Satchmo

The horse, remaining 'on the bit', moves forward with his neck raised and arched. The hocks, being well-engaged, maintain an energetic impulsion, thus enabling the shoulders to move with greater ease in any direction. The horse's steps are shorter than in the other trots, but he is lighter and more mobile. Absolute regularity is maintained throughout all exercises.

In this picture of the legendary German rider, Isabell Werth and her talented partner, Satchmo, the words which immediately spring to mind are 'controlled power', 'ultimate harmony' and 'expression without tension'. These are the same words which describe the qualities that are the essence of the 'art of dressage'.

Although dressage is now one of the most competitive sports in the world, when performed at the highest level, it can be thought of as an art form. A beautifully trained horse, as we see here, has literally been 'sculpted' into 'living art'. Even to the uneducated eye, the sheer beauty of the muscular form horse and rider must make to perform the Grand Prix movements to a high standard, is a joy to behold - just as observing the paintings by the great Masters are a joy.

The technical standpoint from 'the judge's eye' sees Satchmo is well-engaged with very active hindquarters. His well-flexed and supple joints produce the energy that make it so easy for him to come through from behind and 'up' through the shoulders creating the lightness and elasticity that characterize his movements.

In the Grand Prix test the more developed the collected trot is, the more expressive the exercises that are perfomed within it will become, such as the half passes. Great ground covering extensions and instant expressive transitions to passage, for instance, are only possible when the energy and activity of the collected trot is fully developed. One can therefore see the importance that a well executed collected trot, demonstrated with absolute ease and fluency, will have on the overall value of the test. To do well in this sport, horse and rider must master the basic gaits as well as the more advanced elements.

It is equally wonderful to observe Isabell's very good posture - she is sitting deep into the saddle exactly over the centre of gravity of the horse with an extremely supple back and seat. This effective yet supple position enables her to 'energize' Satchmo from behind and yet absorb, rather than 'block', the powerful movement that he produces. Her superb position adds to the total picture of excellence.

Over the years I have had the honour of judging this magnificent combination on several occasions. To witness Satchmo's meteoric rise to fame has been fascinating. From the early days when Isabell first introduced him to international competitions, he was a timid youngster who had to be 'nursed' through scary situations until his trust and faith in his rider outgrew his natural fear of the somewhat artificial surroundings of modern day International Dressage venues.

So popular has this sport become, that the growing number of spectators and generous sponsors expect ringside dining, shopping, loud music and strong lighting, all of which add up to a highly charged atmosphere that these highly-tuned horses must now perform in. However to see this powerful athletic horse now pulling out one supremely confident Grand Prix test after the other is a real testament to Isabell's training and patience. Satchmo has found himself at the top of the International Dressage league table on several occasions. What a thrilling combination to watch and I have a feeling that there is still even more to come.

Isabell Werth

The Rider

My most memorable test

The World Equestrian Games in Aachen 2006 was the turning point for Satchmo. I have had so many wins previously on great partners such as Gigolo, Anthony and Amaretto but this one stands out as one of the best because of the enormous self belief and conviction Satchmo's owner, trainer and I all had in his talent and the long journey it took us to finally gain his confidence so he could perform at his best. It was not just a victory for Satchmo's great talent but a victory for my heart as well that made it so special. We both gave everything we had in that test.

I had intended to take my second horse, the reliable Warum Nicht, to this competition but he was not fit so at the last minute we decided Satchmo would take his place. Because Satchmo can be erratic from one performance to the next, there was less pressure on us to achieve a good result for the team, so I felt I could risk much more that day. No one expected us to win.

As the test went on and we rode from one movement to the next, I kept saying to myself 'this is good', fully expecting Satchmo to explode at any moment, but he didn't. He was so focused the entire time. When we were coming to the end of the test, I knew it was very good - I just wanted to get to the end of it before he had a chance to do something wrong, but he didn't. At the final salute my heart was pounding with excitement, he had performed the most wonderful test. The audience was applauding and screaming. It really didn't matter if we had won or not, Satchmo had just allowed me to ride the most energetic and flowing test. It was such an emotional moment, one I shall never be able to forget.

Above *Isabell Werth winning the Gold medal at Aachen in 2006 - 'what a wonderful day'.*
Opposite, right *Winning the Team Gold medal at the 2006 World Equestrian Games in Aachen, Germany'. l. to r. Nadine Capellmann on Elvis VA, Heike Kemmer on Bonaparte, myself and Hubertus Schmidt on Wansuela Suerte It was a good day for Germany. I also won the Individual Gold medal the next day.*

My Story

1969 I was born 21st July in Rheinberg, GER.

1986 I began to train with Dr. Uwe Schulten-Baumer and remained with him for 16 years.

1988 At 17 I made my International debut at Goodwood in England on Weingart.

2000 I qualified as a lawyer specialising in medical and equine law but soon realised there was not enough time for two demanding careers so I left the firm of Dr Oexmann & Co to focus on riding. My great partner Gigolo retired.

2002 The split from Dr. Uwe Schulten-Baumer was complete. My horses moved to Madeleine Winter-Schulze stables where I trained with Wolfram Wittig. I broke my leg and could not compete for 4 months. Two years later I set up my own yard at my parents farm.

My daily routine

Normally we are showing over the weekend so the horses will have Monday off, which gives me a chance to catch up with paperwork and other matters. I have always had my non-riding enjoyment and interests. I studied law and wrote my exams during the time that I was riding Gigolo. I am also an insatiable reader. One must also be mindful of what is happening around the world and to understand and help support some of the humanitarian issues we are faced with today. It is too easy to become totally focused on what we are doing at the expense of others.

I now have my horses at my parents' farm where I have established my own training yard. Gigolo and the other retired oldies graze in the fields. I ride virtually every day. If the competition horses are resting, I still have the youngsters to ride, which I love to do. It is my greatest joy to see them progress and, if I am honest, it is the reason why I ride. 'Der Doctor', to whom I owe so much, always made riding fun and I try to continue this philosophy in everything I do.

How my riding career began

I started riding when I was five, on a pony called Illa and I am still a member of our local riding club, RV Graft Schmettow Eversael. At 17, the local steel manager and dressage expert, Dr. Uwe Schulten Baumer Sr asked if I would like to ride some of his horses and it was from there that a long and very successful relationship developed.

There are so many ups and downs in this sport and to reach the top requires great support from special people. Madeleine Winter-Schulze never lost faith in my ability and drive to reach the top again after Gigolo retired. It took several years, but together we worked long and hard to nurture the nervous Satchmo's amazing talent and it has paid off. Wolfram Wittig, my trainer, has added balance and stability back to my competitive career. Without Madeleine and Wolfram with their continued support, during good and bad times, my comeback may never have happened.

I will compete for another 10 years, and then, who knows? I have so much to give back to this sport. I would like to use my drive and experiences to make life a little bit better for someone else, if possible. I know how important positive support is to reach your goals and I want to be there for someone else.

My Competition Highlights

1990 Bronze German Championships on Gigolo.

1991 Gold German Championships and Individual and Team Gold at Europeans at Donaueschingen on Gigolo.

1992 Gold, German Championships. Individual Silver and Team Gold Barcelona Olympics on Gigolo, 1st World Cup Finals in Del Mar on Fabienne.

1993 Silver German Championships. Individual and Team Gold at Lipica Europeans on Gigolo.

1994 Individual and Team Gold at FEI World Equestrian Games at Den Haag on Gigolo.

1995 Gold German Championships, Individual and Team Gold at Mondorf Europeans on Gigolo.

1996 Gold German Championships, Team and Individual Gold Atlanta Olympics on Gigolo.

1997 Gold German Championships, Individual and Team Gold at Europeans at Verden on Gigolo.

1998 Gold German Championships, Team and Individual Gold World Equestrian Games in Rome on Gigolo.

1999 Team Gold at Europeans at Arnhem on Gigolo.

2000 Team Gold and Individual Silver at Australian Olympics on Gigolo.

2001 Silver German Championships, Team Gold Europeans at Verden on Anthony.

2003 2nd Grand Prix Kur Stuttgart on Anthony.

2004 1st Grand Prix Special, CSI at Stadl Paura, 2nd Grand Prix Kur at Stuttgart on Anthony.

2006 1st Grand Prix 2nd Kur London on Warum Nicht, 1st Grand Prix Kur on Apache.

2007 Gold Grand Prix and Grand Prix Kur at FEI World Cup Finals Las Vegas on Warum Nicht.

2008 1st Grand Prix at World Cup Final in 's Hertogenbosch on Warum Nicht. 1st Grand Prix and Kur Hamburg on Apache.

2009 2nd Grand Prix and Special at CDI Dortmund on Warum Nicht.

Wolfram Wittig

The Trainer

Above *Wolfram Wittig is not only the trainer of one of the world's best dressage riders but is also a breeder of successful dressage horses*
Opposite top *Boots off and last minute advice for Isabell before entering the arena at Aachen*
Opposite middle *Isabell and Satchmo executing a beautiful half-pass in the warm-up arena at Aachen 2008*
Opposite bottom *Madeleine Winter-Schulze, Satchmo's owner, and Wolfram watch Isabell's test from the side lines*

My Story

1958 I was born in Rahden, Westfalen, Germany.

1971 My interest in horses grows and I begin training with Walter Biedermann for two years.

1986 Brigitte and I marry and move into her father's farm where we take over the operation.

1990 Our breeding programme begins with our first mare producing our foundation stallion Breitling W.

2002 I begin my role as Isabell's trainer. Over the years we develop as a very good team comprising rider, trainer and owner.

2008 Breitling W retires from competiton. Both Brigitte and myself are chosen for the German International B squad along with three of our home bred horses.

Training Isabell and Satchmo

I have been working with Isabell as her trainer since 2002. Unlike her previous 16 year relationship with Dr. Uwe Schulten-Baumer, whom she rode with everyday, I travel to Isabell's stables from my own breeding farm in Westphalia, maybe once or twice each month. However, I attend all of her competitions. Isabell has developed her own successful riding technique and my role is to get the best out of her and Satchmo at competitions. I tell her how it looks for the arena. We also treat situations differently for indoor competitions and outdoor arenas where the lighting, sound and audience movement have an effect on her highly tuned horses and when your aim is to achieve 8s, 9s and 10s you must get the look right. Isabell says I am a great team builder, which I hope is true. At competitions Isabell will take Satchmo out early in the day, hours before she competes, to do her training and to get him used to his environment. He is highly strung and from one moment to the next can explode but he is not a tense or nervous horse which is demonstrated in the beautiful walk he does in the test. After this training session, he will return to his stable where he can relax while Anna grooms and plaits him. About 30 minutes before Isabell enters the test arena, she will bring Satchmo back to the warm up area to concentrate on relaxing and engaging him. It has taken years of patient riding on Isabell's part to get him where he is today but the results show that he is worth it. There are no short-cuts with Satchmo and his behaviour at prize-giving ceremonies is indicative of his training - calm and relaxed.

My own knowledge of dressage is a result of my association with the Spanish Riding School instructor, Walter Biedermann, whom I worked with for two years, Herbert Rehbein, Harry Boldt and Johann Hinnemann.

I have, for many years, bred, trained and competed my own dressage horses. Our stallion, Breitling W, a Hanoverian licensed stallion, rated No. 2 in the German breeding index, was an International Grand Prix challenger and the enormous success we have had with his offspring, confirms our belief in the training methods we use. The horse's mental and physical well-

Wolfram's Competition Highlights

2001 1st Grand Prix, Kur and Team Gold at CDIO Hickstead, Bronze medal German Championships on Breitling W.

2002 5th Grand Prix and Kur Freestyle at Stuttgart, 4th German Championships on Breitling W.

2003 7th World Cup Qualifier at 's Hertogenbosch, 5th Grand Prix Kur at CHIO Aachen on Breitling W.

2004 9th World Cup Qualifier, 7th Grand Prix at Neumunster, 4th German Championships on Breitling W.

2005 4th Grand Prix, 5th Special at Neumunster, 4th German Championships on Breitling W.

2006 Bronze medal at World Championships for Young Dressage Horses in Germany on Biagiotti W.

2007 3rd Grand Prix Special on Charatan W, 2nd Grand Prix Kur at Hagen on Breitling W.

2008 3rd Grand Prix 2nd Kur at CDN Paderborn on Charatan W, 3rd Grand Prix Kur CDN Munster on Berkeley W.

2009 5th Grand Prix 4th Special at CDN Munster on Charatan W.

being is paramount throughout his training and the two must be in harmony if the soul and expression of the horse is to last a lifetime. Our training system emphasises balance in all of the basic paces which will improve self carriage and make training easier for us later on. Of course the natural ability of the horse is important but the capability of the rider is really the deciding factor on how good a horse will be. Unfortunately, not everyone is an Isabell Werth!

Wolfram's secret to success: 'I never look behind me. Whatever successes we have had are in the past, we only look to the future. We thoroughly enjoy all we have when it happens but if I look too much to the past I may find I am part of that history.' **Isabell's secret to success:** 'I have always created a close bond with my horses, not just from riding them, but also by caring for them and loving them everyday. This is my greatest strength as a rider along with my patience'.

Satchmo
The Horse

A day in the life

Satchmo, or Satchie as we call him at home, is a 170cm bay Hanoverian gelding. When I first started to train him, I spent a lot of time on my backside in the sand. He is like an elastic band, so resilient and light - there is only a fine line between victory and disaster with him. He is like a coiled up spring, but it is this strength which gives his movements so much expression. Some say Satchmo is a genius and others that he is mad. You just never know when he will start to rear and act up in a test. But there have been moments of true brilliance, such as when he established a new world record in Stuttgart, that reinforced my belief in him.

There were so many problems with Satchmo at the beginning. I knew he was very talented but there was something inside him that just would not let him perform with the consistency he needed to be really brilliant. In 2005, after an extremely thorough veterinary check-up, it was revealed Satchmo had membranes floating in both eyes that would randomly blur his vision. To a horse this can be a very frightening experience. Following a successful operation and a long recovery, his eye sight was eventually restored and the cause of his erratic behaviour eliminated.

It was shortly after this recovery in 2006 that he did so well at the World Equestrian Games. Correcting his eye

Above *Satchmo just finished one of the best Grand Prix Special tests of his life at Aachen - always alert and ready to go*
Middle *The scoreboard showing Satchmo sets a new World Record for the Grand Prix Special in Stuttgart, 2005 - another indication that he was something special*
Right *Isabell's biggest supporter, Satchmo's owner, Madeleine Winter-Schulze*
Opposite, top *Isabell very pleased with her test and the appreciation of the crowd*
Opposite, bottom *Picturesque but false backdrops are now used in many of the big competition venues*

Satchmo's form

1997 Isabell begins training Satchmo and quickly realises he is very talented, very special and very spooky. Years of riding tests with his unpredictable nature confirmed Isabell's belief in his talent and her patience.

2005 Vets discover floating membranes on Satchmo's eyes and remove them. The appearance of shadows created by the membranes was the main reason for Satchmo's erratic behaviour.

Neuer Weltrekord im
GRAND PRIX
von Isabell Werth
mit Satchmo
79,958%

Satchmo's Competition Highlights

2003 Team Gold Europeans at Hicksted UK, 2nd Grand Prix 3rd Special at CDI Aachen, Silver, German Championships.

2004 1st Grand Prix Special CSI Stadl Paura Austria.

2005 World Record score 79.958% in Grand Prix Special at CDI Stuttgart.

2006 1st Grand Prix Special at World Equestrian Games at Aachen, 1st Grand Prix and Special at CDI Stuttgart, 1st Grand Prix and Special at CDI Hagen, 1st Grand Prix and Special at CDI-W

's Hertogenbosch NL.

2007 Team Silver Individual Gold and Gold in the Grand Prix Kur at European Championships Italy, 1st Grand Prix, Special and Kur at CDIO Aachen.

2008 Team Gold and Gold medal Grand Prix Silver medal Kur at Hong Kong Olympics, 1st Grand Prix Special and Kur at CDIO Aachen, 1st Grand Prix and Special Stuttgart, 1st Grand Prix and Kur CDI-W Frankfurt.

2009 1st Grand Prix Kur CDI-W 's Hertogenbosch, 1st Grand Prix and Kur CDI-W Neumunster, 2nd World Cup Final Las Vegas, 1st Grand Prix and Kur World Dressage Masters.

Satchmo

			Sacramento
		Sandro	Duerte
	Sao Paulo	Gibsey	Gepard
			Wendela
	Lagata		Lanthan
		Legat	Abba
		Sambesi	Seeloewe
			Abkehr

Satchmo was bred by Albert Kambert and was born in 1994. At 2 years old he was purchased by Dr. Schulten-Baumer as a stallion in the Verden sales. Due to his lively nature 'Der Doctor' had him gelded and his training with Isabell began. He is now owned by Madeleine Winter-Schulze and Birgitte Werth but Isabell remains his long term rider.

sight was a major turning point for Satchmo in his competitive dressage career.

At home Satchmo was also very unpredictable before the operation but now he is much calmer and happier. Although Sachie is very gentle, he knows he is a star and expects to be treated like one - he has such a big ego. Anna Kleniuk has been his groom both when he is at home and at shows for many years so his care is very consistent and familiar. He trusts Anna and is always happy when she is around. Inbetween his hectic show schedule Satchie and I spend lots of time hacking out just to relax and to enter a world away from pressurized competitions. He goes out in his field everyday with his friend, who is a goat, or sometimes our small pony. Despite Satchmo's high powered performances he remains very relaxed now.

A great career

Isabell is perhaps the greatest dressage rider ever having won numerous gold medals on several different equine partners such as Fabienne, Gigolo and Warum Nicht at the Olympic Games, World Cup Finals, European Championships, World Equestrian Games and the German National Championships.

Trot Half-Pass

Jan Brink and Bjorsells Briar

The horse should adopt a uniform bend into the direction in which he is moving, with his body becoming almost parallel to the long side of the arena, although the forehand should be fractionally in advance of the hindquarters. The outside legs pass and cross in front of the inside legs. The horse is looking in the direction of which he is moving. He should maintain the same cadence and balance throughout the whole movement. In order to develop the ease and grace of the movement, it is of great importance, not only that the horse is correctly bent, but that this bend is soft, compliant and completely free from resistance, thereby allowing full impulsion to flow easily through the whole body.

Here we see a very typical picture of the elegant and charismatic combination of Swedish rider, Jan Brink and his Swedish Warmblood stallion, Bjorsells Briar. They have become one of the most consistent partnerships to have featured in the top level of the world dressage stage in recent years. This pair have been amongst the top placings in no less than three World Championships, five European Championships, an incredible five World Cup Finals and have represented their country in three Olympic Games at Sydney, Athens and Beijing.

In this picture of Jan and Briar performing the half-pass in trot, we instantly get the feeling of harmony and 'togetherness'. Horse and rider appear to be working almost as one entity. The clarity of each diagonal pair of legs moving in tandem is almost technically perfect and the cadence of the steps manifests itself with a soft and supple spring from one diagonal set of legs to the other.

The compliant and uniform bend that Briar adopts from poll to tail allows the energy to come from the hindquarters and to flow effortlessly through his whole body thereby carrying him forwards with generous ground-covering strides. The carriage and position of the horse's body in a parallel relationship to the long side of the arena is ideal, with his shoulders placed fractionally in advance of his hindquarters, his impulsion and desire to move forwards is not in the least bit disturbed. Jan's

very good position completes the picture. His posture is straight but with relaxed arms and level hands. His hips are also relaxed, allowing the horse to move under him without hindering the cadence or sideways motion of the movement.

Perhaps one of the most delightful features of this picture is the expression on Briar's face, his eyes showing absolute trust, with a true willingness to carry out the wishes of his rider. Such harmony between horse and rider is noticeable and takes a dressage test beyond just being a collection of technically correct movements onto a higher level of ease fluency and expression. This harmony is seen more frequently in longer established relationships between horse and rider where the understanding between them has matured to the point that the rider only needs to use the subtlest of aids. Jan and Briar have been together for many years and demonstrate the highest level of trust and empathy.

To me the half-pass is one of the most elegant and impressive of all the exercises. When executed as perfectly as it is here, it is a demonstration of power with the horse seemingly reaching as far as it can with each stride but moving with the lightness and precision of a ballet dancer. Unlike some other elements of the Grand Prix test the trot half-pass movement is included in all FEI tests from ponies through to the Grand Prix.

Kyra Kyrklund

The Trainer

Our most memorable test

Although Jan has had considerable success with Briar before and after the European Championships in 2003, this was the turning point for them in terms of great performance consistency. We could see changes in Briar during our training the previous week at my stables - he was stronger, more confident and he seemed to know what was required of him. Briar took all of this with him into the arena and performed the most brilliant tests at Hickstead. The audience was so appreciative they gave Jan and Briar a standing ovation - it was truly amazing. Briar just got better and better. He is a wonderful horse and tries so hard for Jan. I would give my heart and soul for this horse.

Training Jan and Briar

Jan and I have the unusual situation in that, not only do I train Jan and Briar, but we also compete against each other in Grand Prix all over the world. We are very good competitors - sometimes he beats me and sometimes I beat him - but we wish each other the best. I suppose what makes training Jan and Briar work so well is that we have a lot in common when it comes to our

Above *Kyra Kyrklund and Max at the World Cup Final. As well as being a professional rider Kyra is also a trainer, author and has her own fashion label.*
Right *Kyra and Jan warming-up before the Grand Prix test at Aachen*
Opposite *Kyra often travels to Jan's yard near Stockholm Sweden for training sessions*

philosophy and understanding of the horse. We both feel riding a 'happy athlete' is the starting point in training. A horse's environment must allow them to move around physically and not just be confined to their stables for twenty or so hours each day. They must also be allowed to communicate with other horses which is so important - basically, it is allowing them to be horses not just competition animals. Jan spends a good deal of time riding all of his horses through the countryside, when they are not competing, as a form of relaxation.

All the training we do is based around pressure and release. The horse must be rewarded instantly and frequently when it has done something right, by releasing the rein or patting them on the neck. If the reward takes longer than 3 seconds to administer you have broken the association link, so you must be quick with your praise.

I have a very pragmatic approach to training as I feel there is no set order to what a horse must learn. Some horses find certain movements and paces naturally easier for them to learn than other movements. If, for instance, a horse can piaffe but finds flying changes

harder then work on the piaffe. As he becomes more balanced and stronger the changes will come - take advantage of his natural abilities. The degree of collection required for piaffe is similar to the collection required for the canter pirouette, teaching one element can make learning another element much easier for the horse. If the horse cannot transfer these skills it would appear to be a training issue rather than the horse's lack of athletic ability.

Jan likes horses which have lots of energy, as it is with Briar, but it is important that the horse remains relaxed. Briar can become tense so we do lots of walking during our training sessions. Jan also works a lot on controlling the length of stride and the speed of the paces. It is not enough to just ask the horse to go forward, the rider must develop the control to determine if going forward means longer strides or quicker strides or both. Developing this control will improve paces overall.

I also believe that a rider has to come out of their comfort zone and encourage the horse out of theirs, from time to time, if they are going to achieve more. Putting pressure on yourself and your horse is not a bad thing, as long as it does not lead to stress. 'If you always do what you always did, you'll always get what you always got. If you are not happy with what you are getting, you have to change what you are doing.'

Above *Briar leaving the arena having just completed his Grand Prix Kur which left him in 7th place with a score of 73% at the CDIO Aachen. During the past decade Jan and Briar have consistently placed in the top ten in international competitions*
Opposite *Briar and Jan performing medium trot against the beautiful floral decorations surrounding the judges boxes at Aachen*

Bjorsells Briar 899

The Horse

A day in the life

Briar is a 17hh long-legged liver chestnut stallion, with a passion for people. Briar is instantly recognizable by his big white face and three white socks. Elegant but powerful, Briar is one of the most, if not THE most, popular dressage horse of the decade.

From the time he was a young foal, Briar was destined for competitive greatness. His wonderful temperament, a trademark he passes down to his offspring, coupled with his natural dressage talent, played an important part in his induction to International Grand Prix dressage at the very young age of eight - a feat several of his ancestors on his mother's side have also achieved.

In his capacity as a breeding stallion, his season normally runs from mid-March to August. Somehow he is able to separate the breeding mentality from his focused competition mindset - a difficult task for most stallions but one which assures his continuous competitive greatness.

Briar has spent his entire competitive and breeding life with me at Tullstorp in Sweden. I am very mindful of a stallion's natural curiosity and have designed a circular barn, so Briar and the other stallions can see everything going on from their stables.

Briar is a magic horse and if I look back in time I strongly feel one of my biggest accomplishments with him is that I have managed him well, enabling him to keep the drive and mental freshness towards his competitions throughout all the years. At home in his stable and at shows he is very calm and relaxed. He does not spend his energy worrying or becoming nervous instead he uses this energy and power for the competition. At competitions, once he is settled in his new stable, he will often lie down and go to sleep. Even two hours before he is due in the arena he can be sound asleep. At home he is out of his stable at least three times a day, going on the walker, out on hacks and training. I find I get a much better response from him at shows, if I treat him like a horse at home. We spend a lot of time hacking through the forest, along small roads, on the race track or just standing and looking around. I try not to override him at home or to spend too much time on technical work as he already knows how to do everything. The exercises we do are more to keep him in good condition, fit and motivated. Briar likes carrots and apples, which he gets lots of and he particularly likes to put his head on my shoulder when I am talking to him. He is such a gentle horse and it hard to believe sometimes that he is a stallion.

During breeding season, he goes for collection on the farm three times a week - Monday, Wednesday and Friday. This has been part of his normal regime for many years and he approaches his stallion duties with the same relaxed nature as he conducts the rest of his life. Fortunately many of his offspring have inherited his calm, sensible nature along with his easy aptitude for piaffe and passage. But many of his offspring also have his energy and power in competitions, which makes them more suitable for professional riders. At the moment Briar has eight approved sons who are

Briar's Competition Highlights

1996 2nd 5yo Swedish Breeders Trophy.

1997 3rd 6yo Swedish Breeders Trophy.

2000 Team member at Sydney Olympics.

2001 7th World Cup Final at Vilhelmsborg, Swedish National Champion, Swedish Horse of the Year, ranked world No.1 Dressage Stallion.

2002 13th at World Equestrian games in Jerez, 1st Stockholm Grand Prix and Special, 6th World Cup Final at s'Hertogenbosch, Swedish National Champion.

2003 Individual Silver European Championships at Hickstead, 1st Stockholm Grand Prix and Special, 9th World Cup Final at Goteborg, Swedish National Champion.

2004 1st Norten-Hardenberg Grand Prix and Special.

2005 Swedish National Champion, Double Bronze European Championships, 1st Grand Prix and Kur at CDIO Aachen.

2006 7th Grand Prix at Aachen, Swedish National Champion.

2007 1st Grand Prix and Kur at World Cup Qualifier at Stockholm, Team Bronze European Championships, 5th Grand Prix and Kur at World Cup Final in Las Vegas.

2008 2nd Grand Prix 1st Kur at CDI Flyinge, 5th World Cup Final at 's Hertogenbosch, 5th Team Beijing Olympics, Swedish National Champions.

2009 1st Grand Prix and Kur at CDI-W Goteborg, 8th Grand Prix at World Cup Final in Las Vegas, Briar retires from international competition.

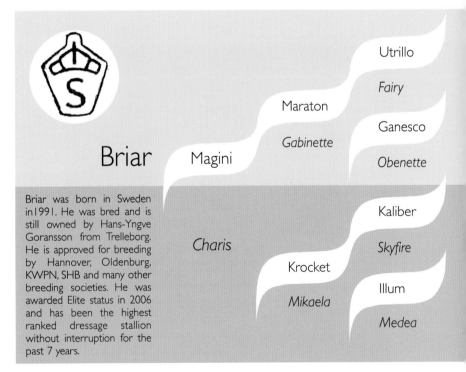

Briar

Briar was born in Sweden in 1991. He was bred and is still owned by Hans-Yngve Goransson from Trelleborg. He is approved for breeding by Hannover, Oldenburg, KWPN, SHB and many other breeding societies. He was awarded Elite status in 2006 and has been the highest ranked dressage stallion without interruption for the past 7 years.

Briar	Magini	Maraton	Utrillo
			Fairy
		Gabinette	Ganesco
			Obenette
	Charis	Krocket	Kaliber
			Skyfire
		Mikaela	Illum
			Medea

competing from S level up to Grand Prix, with many of them having received 10s for their rideability and quality of gaits. In addition, many of his offspring are excellent jumpers.

Briar is now eighteen years old and has completed more than 100 Grand Prix in his competitive career. My partner of ten years is showing no signs of slowing down but it is time for him to stop and enjoy a well deserved retirement.

Training Briar at home

Briar, for a breeding stallion and competition horse, is so relaxed. Jan attributes his good state of mind to the fact that they spend so much of their time, in between shows, at home riding out around the farm and using the fields to do their training. Jan claims this routine keeps Briar interested in competing, because he is not training everyday in the arena and it allows him to really unwind from the hectic pace of travelling to competitions all over the world. Jan's understanding of Briar's needs has been instrumental in the stallions long term success against a field of strong international competitors. In the world dressage rankings Briar has remained in the elite top ten for most of his competitive life. At the 2009 World Cup Final in Las Vegas, Jan and Briar performed in front of an audience for the last time. Briar returned to Tullstorp Stables in Sweden to enjoy a much deserved retirement from competitions. He will continue to fulfil his stallion duties.

Tullstorp Dressage Stable
An aerial view of Tullstorp Dressage Stable was established in 1981 by Jan Brink and Bruno Albinsson in Hassleholm Sweden. From humble beginnings it has developed into a training facility for international competition horses and it has become one of Sweden's most important breeding centres. There is a strong focus at Tullstorp on the breeding and training of the modern sport horse including dressage, jumping and racing. Uncompromising excellence is the key to the high standards practised at the centre

Extended Trot

Nadine Capellmann and Farbenfroh

The horse covers as much ground as possible. Maintaining the same tempo as the collected trot, he lengthens his steps to the utmost as a result of impulsion from the hindquarters. The rider allows the horse, whilst remaining 'on the bit', to lengthen his frame and gain as much ground as possible. The forefeet should touch the ground on the spot at which they are pointing. The movement of the fore and hind legs of each diagonal pair should be well matched (parallel) in the forward movement of the extension. The movement should be well balanced with the transition to the extended trot being rhythmic and well marked. The return to the collected trot should be smoothly executed by taking more weight on the hindquarters without any loss or alteration of rhythm.

In this impressive picture of the former World Champions, Nadine Capellmann and Farbenfroh, we can easily see why they were able to dominate the World dressage stage at the beginning of this century. In this illustration we are given the impression of total commitment in this 'full powered' extended trot. This combination took the risk when it really mattered and could produce 'high voltage' performances that had everyone sitting on the edge of their seats.

Nadine's ability to produce this beautiful and highly volatile horse for the arena was admirable indeed. To manage to remain in control, but still ride with maximum impulsion with such a lightness of footfall is what often gave her the edge over her rivals.

Farbenfroh's ability to cover the absolute maximum amount of ground with each majestic stride as shown here, whilst maintaining perfect balance and straightness with each step matching the next from the start of the diagonal line to the end, is what allowed him to achieve the maximum scores. His fluent and rhythmic transitions, both from collected to extended paces and back again excelled.

In this picture the rider's elegant position in the saddle with this lovely forward contact from the hands, thereby allowing her horse to perform to his utmost, completes this beautiful image of harmony and expression that is rare to see. Farbenfroh was easily identified by his big white face and four generous white socks which almost appeared to highlight his movement.

Nadine and her trainer Klaus Balkenhol understood this horse completely and were able to take the very motivated Farbenfroh through the scales of training keeping him relaxed and confident and thus encouraging the expressive movement he possessed naturally. Nadine had a very special relationship with the sometimes difficult Farbenfroh and together they were able to climb to the top of the International Dressage scene in no time at all. Farbenfroh will always be remembered for his creative performances in the Kur where his footfall to the Greek music was precise.

It was a very sad day indeed for the dressage world when we learned that Farbenfroh had not recovered from a medical operation. There are many successful combinations in this sport but there are not many which possessed the colour, talent and expression that Farbenfroh did - he was so enthusiastic. Nadine has fortunately found a new partner and is once again moving up the ranks in International Dressage.

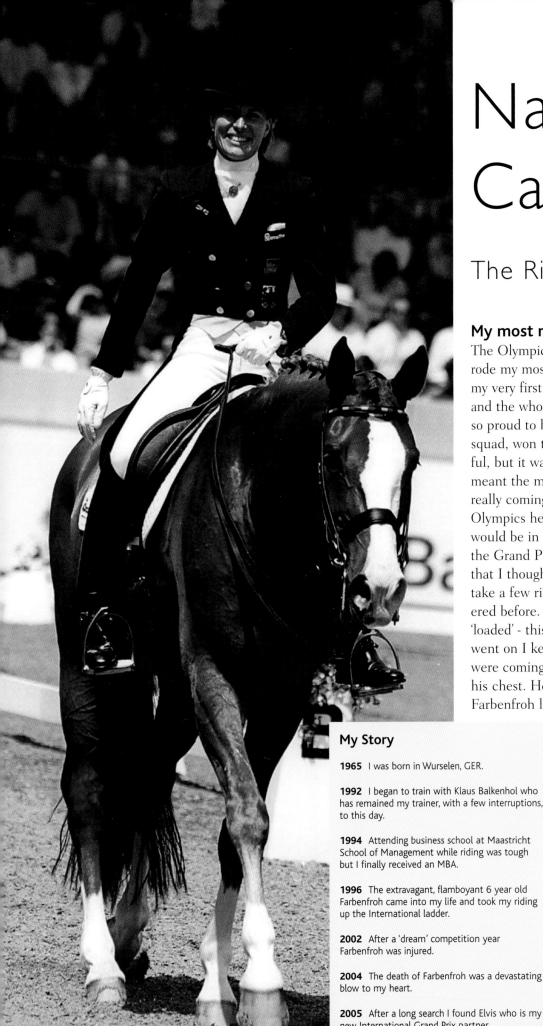

Nadine Capellmann

The Rider

My most memorable test

The Olympic games at Sydney in 2000 was where I rode my most memorable test on Farbenfroh. This was my very first Olympics and the parades, the stadium and the whole atmosphere was very, very exciting. I was so proud to be part of it all. My team, the German squad, won the Gold medal that day which was wonderful, but it was Farbenfroh's performance which really meant the most to me. He was now ten years old and really coming into his own. A few weeks before the Olympics he was working really well so I knew we would be in good shape for the big event. On the day of the Grand Prix team test, our preparations went so well that I thought I could really push him to the limit and take a few risks, something I would never have considered before. When we entered the arena he was so 'loaded' - this was not going to be a safe test. As the test went on I kept looking down at his neck and his knees were coming up so high they were almost banging into his chest. He was being so expressive and showing off. Farbenfroh liked the big Olympic audience of almost 20,000 and was doing his best to impress them. We came fourth overall, but the score that day didn't matter to me. We were in a big event and Farbenfroh showed me that he could do his best. This was an attitude he seemed to establish at these Olympic Games - the bigger the show, the more expressive his performance would be.

My daily routine

At home I normally will have six horses to ride every day. There is only myself and my groom Sabine Domhöfer, who

My Story

1965 I was born in Wurselen, GER.

1992 I began to train with Klaus Balkenhol who has remained my trainer, with a few interruptions, to this day.

1994 Attending business school at Maastricht School of Management while riding was tough but I finally received an MBA.

1996 The extravagant, flamboyant 6 year old Farbenfroh came into my life and took my riding up the International ladder.

2002 After a 'dream' competition year Farbenfroh was injured.

2004 The death of Farbenfroh was a devastating blow to my heart.

2005 After a long search I found Elvis who is my new International Grand Prix partner.

has been with me since 1999, on the yard so we always have much to do. Sabine is a very competent and knowledgeable groom, who was fortunate enough to train with the great Reiner Klimke and Margite Otto-Crepin. She is extremely kind towards horses which is important to me. Sabine also attends all of the shows with me, so her presence is a vital part of the machinery that keeps us organised.

At some point I would love to do more training of my own young horses at home and perhaps not do so much competing. In my spare time, I love to cook for friends

and I also collect art, which I am very interested in. I am very conscious of the growing need to be more sympathetic towards our environment and towards less fortunate people so I have charities that I like to support with my time. At competitions I have a set routine which I do

to prepare myself mentally for each test. After Farbenfroh and my early morning training sessions and before I am due in the arena I will sleep for up to two hours. I have always had this routine.

How my riding career began

Being the daughter of an international dressage rider, it was inevitable that if I was going to ride at all, it would be dressage. My father, Kurt Capellmann, who competed in the 1940s and 50s, went so far as to hide all the jumping poles when my sister, Gina and myself were little so we wouldn't be tempted to follow a career of jumping or eventing. My love of animals is a big of part of why I started riding and why I still ride today. I also have a dream of winning the Olympic Individual Gold medal. I have won the Olympic Team Gold medal twice but so far the individual medal has eluded me. I had ridden for many years and was doing okay before Farbenfroh came along but he took my riding up to a new level. We were now challenging the world's best and at times beating them. To ride such a talented horse was an amazing experience, but all too brief.

Opposite *Nadine Capellmann and the fabulous Farbenfroh leaving the arena at Aachen 2002 after the Grand Prix Kur which they won*
Above *Nadine and Farbenfroh in an elegant trot half-pass at Aachen*
Left *Nadine giving an interview immediately after winning the Grand Prix Kur. With dressage growing in popularity the media are present at all of the 'big' shows ready to interview the winners for radio and television*

Klaus Balkenhol

The Trainer

Above *Klaus Balkenhol*
Opposite, top *Nadine and Farbenfroh in medium trot*
Opposite, right *Klaus, Nadine and Nadine's groom Sabine Domhöfer sorting out the bridle on of Nadine's young horses, Raffaldo, before the warm up begins at Aachen 2009. Klaus has been involved training Nadine and her horses for over twenty-five years*

Training Nadine and Farbenfroh

I received a call from a young man who had Farbenfroh and believing he was a good horse, wanted to sell him. Nadine and I went to see him and she fell in love with Farbenfroh instantly and bought him. During his early training Farbenfroh stayed with me. Nadine and I had worked together for many years already so we had an understanding as to the direction his training would take. The art of this training was simply not to over challenge him as he was so willing to perform, you had to be careful not to over tax him. He had everything a good dressage horse should have - all the basic paces were there along with a very good passage and piaffe. He had to be exemplary otherwise he would not have become a world champion. Farbenfroh was very lucky he had Nadine as his rider. He was so motivated and very sensitive and Nadine empathized with this - which was clear to see, there was never disharmony between them. Nadine is an unbelievably good competition rider, who always thinks of her horse. One must try, as an individual, to get into the horse's mind, the horse should not have to adapt to the rider. Nadine was very aware of this with Farbenfroh and ensured he maintained his character. They worked very hard together which is why they were able to win the Team Gold at Sydney and Individual Gold at the WEG.

Along with many other trainers, I believe in and teach the classical method of dressage, which means following the scales of training - rhythm, suppleness, contact, impulsion, straightness and collection. I also believe that if the horse and rider can develop a method of relaxation then these principles can be demonstrated with more expression. There are many new methods and techniques of training bandied about at the moment but I do feel we will once again revert to the classical system which has the happiness and well being of the horse in the forefront. The horse is not trained to be a slave but a partner. I know the classical system works because I have trained my own horses to Grand Prix level using this method and it is easy to see the impressive international results of both Goldstern and Rabauke. As I am now a trainer of many international Grand Prix riders, their successes are also a

My Story

1939 Born 6th Dec at Velen, Germany, my passion for horses began at an early age on my parents farm.

1979 I contacted the German National Equestrian Federation, as a virtual unknown, requesting to be considered for the German Olympic squad. Shortly after we were ranked No.1 in the world but my horse Rabauke was injured just before the Olympics.

1981 Goldstern was assigned to the Dusseldorf police force where I commenced his training both as a police horse and dressage horse.

1991 - 1996 We won the German National title, Goldstern and I rose to the International arena.

1996 Goldstern retired, I became trainer to top International riders and the US Olympic Team.

2003 I was bestowed with the 'Horseman of the Year Dressage' award from the USA.

Klaus' Competition Highlights

1979 2nd German National Champions in Berlin on Rabauke.

1990 German National Champion in Munster on Goldstern.

1991 German National Champion, Team Gold medal at European Championships in Munster on Goldstern.

1992 German National Champion, Team Gold and Individual Bronze at Barcelona Olympics on Goldstern.

1993 German National Champion, Team Gold at European Championships in Lipica, 1st Grand Prix in Stuttgart, 1st Grand Prix Special in Dusseldorf, 1st World Cup Qualifier in Amsterdam and Berlin, 1st Grand Prix, 1st Grand Prix Kur in Stuttgart on Goldstern.

1994 Team Gold and Individual Silver FEI World Equestrian Games, The Hague, 1st Grand Prix in Bremen, 1st World Cup Qualifier in Neumunster; 1st Grand Prix Special Steinhagen on Goldstern.

1995 German National Champion in Gera, Team Gold at European Championships in Mondorf, 1st Grand Prix in Steinhagen, 1st Grand Prix Special in Berlin on Goldstern.

1996 German National Champion, Team Gold at Atlanta Olympics, 1st Grand Prix and Special in Olfen on Goldstern. Goldstern is retired from competition.

testament to the solid foundations the classical system instils. At the WEG at Jerez, in Spain, I was the trainer for seven competitors from three different countries. My private students included half of the German team who won the Gold medal and I was the official coach of the USA team who won the Bronze medal. It was also on this occasion that Nadine and Farbenfroh won the Individual Gold medal.

The best trainers I have had are the horses themselves. With them I have tried to make a mistake only once - but I didn't always succeed. In the beginning, as a policeman, I had no money for dressage lessons so I had to feel my way forward with piaffe, passage and the flying changes. The horses showed me what was good but also what was bad. It was my Chief of Mounted Police who had worked with George Wahl who told me you should always think of a horse as a friend and partner - then you will win him over and the horse will give you everything. This is a principle that I have always adhered to.

Now that I am retired from the police force, my farm is continually busy with riders and horses who come for training from all over the world. I also travel extensively, in particular to the United States, as I was coach of the US Olympic Team from 2000 to 2008. If I did not have the support of my wife, Judith, this just would not be possible and now that my daughter, Annabel, is competing at Grand Prix, it is good to be home more often.

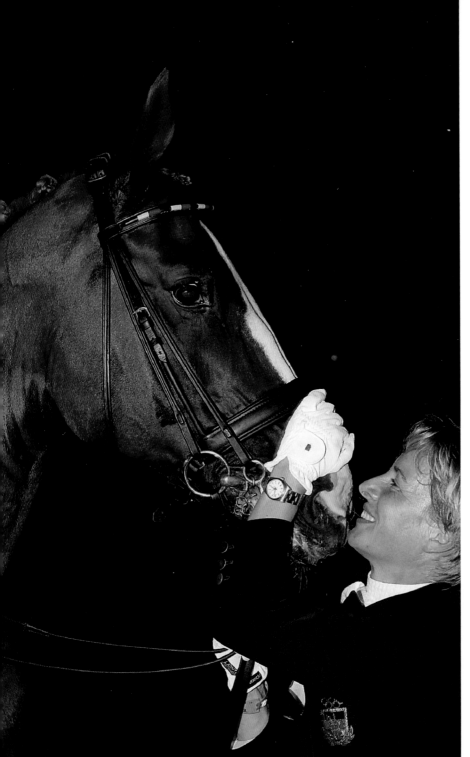

Farbenfroh

The Horse

A day in the life

Where does one begin with Farbenfroh. 'Farbenfroh' means colour-gladly or happy colours which suited him perfectly. We referred to him as the 'multi-coloured fox' and gave him the nickname 'Schnuckel'. He was flamboyant, his movements extravagant, he was a genius, he was mad, he was beautiful. He was a 'once in a lifetime' horse. I first met him when he was five - already his movements were awesome - exaggerated by his big white face and his four white socks. So natural were his piaffe and passage movements, that at the age of only eight, he competed in his first Grand Prix Special and won. His personality was as big as his movements and this came across to the spectators and judges who loved to watch him. He was always on the edge, his ears constantly up and alert - this happy horse totally enjoying himself. The German crowds voted him 'Horse of the Year' an honour which was bestowed upon him in front of a full house at Aachen. He was the epitomy of the 'happy athlete' which is a big concern in modern dressage. From one test to the next he could set a new world record and give me the ride of giants and then, in the next test, decide he would not even go into the arena. He was an absolute handful to train and live with but the rewards of owning and riding such a talented, talented horse were enormous. I knew from very early on that having Farbenfroh would take me up the international ladder of success. At the beginning of his competition life Farbenfroh was more consistent in his nature but one day when we were at a big show in Hamburg, the stewards had to remove a chain across the entrance of the arena each time a competitor entered or left. As Farbenfroh and I were entering the arena this chain was on the ground and just as Farbenfroh put his foot on it, the steward pulled on the chain, which made him jump. Since that time Farbenfroh would always look at the ground waiting for the 'snake' to appear.

At home his big personality took over. He knew exactly what he wanted and would somehow always achieve his goal to receive extra sweets and attention. Despite

---

Farbenfroh's Competition Highlights

1996 1st German Young Horse Championship in 6yr old division.

1998 1st Grand Prix Special, local show.

1999 1st Grand Prix Special, 2nd Grand Prix Aachen, 7th Grand Prix Stuttgart.

2000 1st Grand Prix Special, 4th Grand Prix Aachen, 3rd Grand Prix Special Stuttgart, 4th Individual, Team Gold at Sydney Olympics.

2001 Team Gold, Individual Bronze European Championships, Gold German National Championships with a World Record score of 78.72% in Grand Prix.

2002 Team and Individual Gold at World Equestrian Games in Jerez Spain, 1st Grand Prix Kur at Aachen.

his happy exterior, he was very wary of strangers and would often bite anyone he did not know. My small yard suited Farbenfroh as he was very comfortable with Sabine and myself and trusted us totally - the whole yard eventually revolved around him.

After our fantastic double Gold medal at the World Equestrian Games in Spain, where Farbenfroh gave me the best ride of his life, he pulled a tendon. We decided to give him a long rest to recuperate slowly and completely. In total, he had 15 months off before we started competing again. Farbenfroh was now 14 years old and the comeback was very difficult. During one of our training sessions he mis-stepped and became lame again. This time we opted for him to have a simple operation on his front legs in December 2004. As he was coming out of the anaesthetic, he fell over in the recovery box and broke his leg so severely, there was no chance of recovery. I made the most painful decision of my life to have him humanely put to sleep. His death has left the most enormous hole in my heart and in my life. After a very long search I have found another very talented horse to ride, but there will never be another horse like Farbenfroh.

Farbenfroh

Farbenfroh was born in Germany in 1990 from a Westphalian father and a Trakehner mother. He was bought by Nadine in 1996 when he was six years old and stayed with Nadine until his sad, untimely death in 2004. His sire has produced over 100 competition horses but to date Farbenfroh remains his most famous offspring.

			Fruehling
		Fruehlingstraum II	Abendkind
	Freudentaenzer	Simona	Sioux
			Roxane
			Aar
Anuschka	Aarstein		Fanny
	Baccarai		Bengale
			Severine

Opposite *Farbenfroh and a very happy Nadine after winning the Gold medal at the World Equestrian Games in Jerez de la Frontera in Spain in 2002*
Below *Although Farbenfroh had energetic paces Nadine was able to keep him relaxed and flowing as this picture shows*

Nadine Capellmann and Farbenfroh

Farbenfroh performing one of his amazing passage - piaffe tours at the CHIO in Aachen, Germany 2002. In this competition Farbenfroh placed second in the Grand Prix behind Ulla Salzgeber on Rusty but in the Grand Prix Kur Farbenfroh won the class. All of Farbenfroh's paces were extravagant matched only by his larger than life personality. The death of Farbenfroh in 2004, due to a recurring leg injury was an immense loss to Nadine and the dressage world.

Collected Canter

Coby van Baalen and Ferro

The horse, remaining 'on the bit' moves forward with cadence. The neck is raised and arched. The hocks, being well-engaged, maintain an energetic implusion, enabling the shoulders to move with greater mobility, thus demonstrating self-carriage and an uphill tendency. The horse's strides are shorter than in the other canters without losing elasticity and cadence.

Here we see a fascinating shot of the dynamic black stallion Ferro with his charming and beautiful rider, Coby van Baalen. This pair have achieved so much during their illustrious career and are probably most famous for their breathtaking Piaffe/Passage tour that brought a lump to many spectators throats, even to some of the judges! Their partnership was so complete and almost unique, it was truly emotional to watch them in action.

In this 'Collected Canter Right' we can see the beginning of the true canter sequence with the outside (left) hind leg starting the motion, the outside diagonal (left fore and right hind) about to reach the ground simultaneously, and then finally the inside (right) fore finishing the 'three beat time' of the canter sequence, with all joints correctly bent, emphasizing the expression of the canter itself. Following this will be the moment of suspension and then the whole 'three time' sequence will begin again.

The feeling of real concentration can be seen both in Coby's elegant and well-balanced position in the saddle and Ferro's facial expression with his ears tilted slightly towards his rider, as if 'listening' to her every command and waiting for the next one. As a stallion, Ferro could be forgiven if he was distracted but he was always focused on Coby when in the arena. If mares are also competing it can turn the head of any breeding stallion making them difficult to control.

Having come to Coby from a jumping background, he and Coby climbed the ranks of International Grand Prix dressage very quickly due to Ferro's enormous talent, Coby's skilful riding and the expert knowledge of her trainer, Johann Hinnemann. Together they represented Holland in every major dressage event with enormous success. The main ingredient in Ferro's success was that Coby and Johann took time to understand Ferro and to get Ferro to focus on his work. It took over a year of patient handling before Ferro looked to Coby for praise and attention. Once this happened, they grew into the talented partnership that became firm favourites on the dressage stage. In his relatively short competition career, brought to an end due to a leg injury, Ferro accomplished so much and was a strong member of many Dutch International Teams.

Coby's affections for Ferro continued long after his competitive career was over. With a busy breeding schedule ahead of him, she assigned a full-time groom to attend to him alone so that he would receive all the care and attention he had grown used to during his competitive life. Unfortunately due to a severe collick attack his life was cut short.

Fortunately the talent and superb conformation of this amazing black stallion has been passed on to many of his progeny who are also now competing in the highest levels of dressage and jumping.

Above *The demure and elegant Coby van Baalen deep in concentration riding BMC Ojay at the World Cup Final in 's Hertogenbosch 2008*
Right *Winning the Team Silver medal with Arjen Teeuwissen, Chef d'equipe Jurgen Koschel, Anky van Grunsven and Ellen Bontje at the Australian Olympics 2000*

Coby van Baalen
The Rider

My most memorable test
It was the last selection trial to make the Dutch team which would represent Holland at the World Equestrian Games in Rome. It was held at the CHIO at Rotterdam in 1998. I was tied for 5th place with Sven and Gonnelien Rothenberger. The Grand Prix class was very big so it was held over two days and I was scheduled to ride on the second day. I had no idea what the scores were for the previous day, I only knew that I was going to go all out in this test. My warm up went well and my concentration was very good. We had done everything possible to be ready for this test, Ferro was on form and I was too. During the test we made a few mistakes but I didn't dwell on this. I just went for it from the beginning till I left the arena at the end. The whole test just flowed. We had a score of over 72 per cent, which was a high score then and good enough to make the team - I was on top of the world.

My daily routine
My days are always busy so we start very early in the morning and just keep going. Working with horses is my hobby, my passion - I do it with love so the long hours do not bother me. I now have my daughter Marlies and my niece Marrigje to help with the running of our farm Dressage Van Baalen. Both Marlies and Marrigje compete at international events, which is good to show off the stallions and it takes the pressure off me to do so much riding and with their experiences they also help with teaching the many students who come to our farm, many of whom are on international squads for ponies, juniors and young riders. I love working with the stallions

My Story

1957 I was born 6th April in Werkhoven Holland.

1975 My future husband, Arie, and I met at a breeders show.

1978–1990 To save money we lived with Arie's parents in a caravan while Arie ran his large dairy business and I established Dressage Van Baalen.

1980–1984 Marlies and Arie Jr. were born and the family is complete.

1998 Ferro came into my life and together with training from Johann Hinneman we rose to the top of the international dressage world.

2009 I look back with fondness at all of the training I did with Johann on Ferro and even today my greatest pleasure is to train young horses with Johann Hinneman.

but I also love teaching and I must confess I now spend most of my time teaching these days. When I am not working with the horses I run half marathons to keep fit, I cherish my house and gardens and I like to read a good book - but this does not happen very often.

How my riding career began

I did not come from a family with horses but I always loved horses and wanted so much to have a career with them. My family thought otherwise and encouraged me instead to become a florist. I started training full time but gradually the horses took over and I finally left the florist business behind to pursue my dream. It was while I was giving riding lessons that I met my husband Arie van Baalen. Although his family ran a large dairy operation, his father also owned several broodmares. He encouraged his son to learn to ride and it was while I was teaching Arie to ride that we fell in love and married. It was not an easy start for us. We wanted to save money to build up Arie's dairy business and my riding business so we lived in a caravan on Arie's parents estate for twelve years. When the children arrived, Arie's parents were also very willing baby-sitters. It was Arie's father who encouraged me to buy a little horse called Natrial. I also started training in dressage with Henk van Bergen. It was due to the successes I had with Natrial in Prix St Georges that people started bringing their horses to me for training and my business grew. In 1981, Henk van Tuyl brought me his stallions

Coby's Competition Highlights

2001 3rd Dutch Championships in Nijmegen with Welt Hit II, 1st Kur in Maastricht with Welcome.

2003 Coby receives the 'Goldenes Reiterabzeichen' in Wardendorf for high achievement presenting the Wardendorf stallions.

2005 1st Stallion Show in Zwolle with BMC Kigali, 4th Dutch Championships Nijmegen with BMC Kigali.

2006 5th Grand Prix CHIO Rotterdam with BMC Kigali.

2007 1st Grand Prix in Uden with BMC Ojay, 2nd Grand Prix Gelderland with BMC Ojay, 1st Grand Prix and Special CDI Oldenburg with BMC Ojay.

Uddel and Ulft (Ferro's sire) to train and show. We won the Dutch Championships which encouraged more people to bring their stallions to me for training as I seemed to be developing the reputation as someone who got on well with stallions. In 1989 I began having lessons with Johann Hinnemann and together we trained my first Grand Prix ride, Biraldo. It was from here that my small business turned into 'Dressage Stable Van Baalen' with 25 boxes, indoor arena, canteen, solarium, tack room, and facilities for stallions and broodmares and finally - our own house. We trained many good stallions here such as Idocus, Fidermark and Welt Hit II.

In 1998 I had one of my stallions, Inspekteur, at the same stallion station as Ferro. I noticed Ferro immediately because he was so beautiful. He had not accomplished much in the jumping or dressage disciplines at that time but I expressed an interest in training him and, as luck would have it, he arrived at my stables for training and shortly after we stormed the international Grand Prix scene. This was the nicest time of my life.

After Ferro I had a lovely promising colt called Pasternak which I bred myself from Gribaldi. He was so talented and started his Grand Prix career at the age of nine, getting scores over 70 per cent. He was definitely destined to become a top world class dressage horse. Sadly he was stricken with a virus after a competition in Dortmund and died as a result. That was the most traumatic period in my life ever, to lose Ferro and then Pasternak.

Today I have given the ride on my Jazz offspring, BMC Ojay, to my daughter. Ojay and I were on the Dutch National B squad and now Marlies has found herself on the B squad with him as well. I consider Marlies' career more important than my own now. I shall definitely be in the background bringing on the young horses for Marlies to ride. She has the discipline and the will power to make it to the top. And she knows that if you want something you can achieve it, with hard work of course. I have had the most wonderful experiences competing at the Olympics, the World Equestrian Games and the European Champions in the Grand Prix and the Kurs - I have been very lucky and now it is Marlie's turn.

Johann Hinnemann

The Trainer

Above *Johann Hinneman watching his students warming up at the CHIO Aachen* **Opposite** *Coby and Johann have worked together for many years training and showing dressage horses and ponies. They have enjoyed innumerable successes*

My Story

1948 I was born 29th August in Lower Voerde, Holland.

1968 For 4 years I studied with Reiner Klimke and Gunter Guminski to obtain my Bereiter.

1972 Gisela and I married and over the years our family grows to include a daughter and a son.

1981 I was coach of the Canadian National Dressage Team for 5 years.

1997 Along with Klaus Balkenhol, I was coach of the German National Team.

1998 I was awarded the Trainer of the Year status by the International Dressage Trainers Club.

2003 Along with Sjef Janssen, I was coach of the Dutch A squad.

Teaching Coby and Ferro

I have been working with Coby since 1988. An American student of mine, Dennis Collin, was in Holland looking for horses to buy and he met Coby. She expressed that she needed some help with a few of her horses so he suggested she get in touch with me and that is how it all started and we are still together. 'Trainer' is not a term that I like to use when describing my relationship with Coby, we are more like business partners. Together we have produced more than 15 Grand Prix horses but Ferro was the most popular. Our relationship has worked and stood the test of time because we are both crazy about horses, we have an eye for the same type of horses and together we accomplish more than 110%. With Coby's competitive career she relied on me because I stood behind her through all of the good and bad tests. I have been lucky enough to have competed myself in every major competition arena throughout the world so I know how it feels to perform at these high levels and these experiences helped me with all my students. On the other side, there is more to Coby and I than piaffe, passage and flying changes, we are both interested in breeding. Coby is from a breeding background as her father bred horses and her father-in-law was one of the most popular horsemen in the Netherlands. We go together to look at and buy horses, Coby rides them and we sell them. Our daughters knew each other and initially they were both riding. Marlies decided to become a professional rider and my daughter became a veterinarian specializing in embryo transplants. There was no chance that Marlies would train anywhere but my place, so the association with the van Baalen family continues. Now the business extends over both our farms. Marlies trains Pony Riders, Coby, the Junior and Young Riders. I do most of the training of the young horses so we always have a large selection of good horses for our growing group of young riders. Altogether we have 10 to 12 horses that are on the International Junior and Young Rider squads such as Roman Nature, Revino and Don Cardinale. At the Dutch Nationals one year we had about 10 horses competing initially. With so many students at the same show, we need both Coby and myself on the ground to make it work and this is where our team organization shows.

Coby has always worked with stallions, particularly young stallions, so it was no surprise that she got on so well with Ferro. When Ferro first came to us, he was supposed to be working at Prix St Georges level, but one could see that Ferro needed much more training to do the job properly. Coby loved him from the start because he was beautiful, sensitive and very strong, she knew he would take her all the way to the top of the international dressage world. At some competitions Coby and Ferro can feel the pressure so we try to find a quiet corner to focus on the test. Over the years of getting to know Ferro, Coby has found that doing short bursts of the piaffe in the warm-up was the best way to get him to concentrate on her and not be dazzled by or curious of the big crowds.

I like horses which are very strong and supple in the back. First I have to see if the horse can jump because this will show if they use their back correctly. The eyes of a horse will tell you a lot about their interior. They have to be intelligent and be able to relate to people. By this I mean they have to react to people and be interested in people. It is so much easier to train a horse who looks for rewards from people. Ferro was easy to train because he was so intelligent, always willing to work and because he trusted and respected me.

A good rider these days must also be very athletic and willing to work hard. Right from Ponies through to Grand Prix I insist that all my students go on a fitness regime. Competitions are very hard to win and riders have to be fitter than ever.

Although I was trained in the classical way, I do have great appreciation for different techniques of riding that bring results. The systems we teach are for everyday horses and riders. The exceptional horses and top experienced riders can add a little extra to the techniques that makes them a little bit different. In a way they are artists and we have to allow them this expression as long as the wellbeing of the horse is not jeopardized.

I still ride everyday and I do not miss the competing as I get so much enjoyment teaching and training young horses and when they do well at competitions it means a lot. I was brought up to be a professional instructor and this is what I love to do. During the time

Johann's Competition Highlights

1986 Team Gold Individual Bronze World Championships Toronto Canada, Team Gold at CDIO Lausanne, Team Gold CHIO at Donaueschingen on Ideaal.

1987 Team Gold Individual Bronze at European Championships Goodwood

England, Team Gold CHIO in Aachen on Ideaal.

2000 As team trainer to Coby van Baalen and Ferro, Alexandra Simons de Ridder and Chacomo, Ulla Salzgeber and Rusty and Christine Traurig and Etienne they came 3rd, 5th 7th and 10 respectively at the Sydney Olympics. Although these riders competed for different countries the camaradarie was amazing.

I was competing, many competitions were closed to professional riders like myself, such as the Olympics and many of the big FEI events. In order to take part I had to become an amateur and say good-bye to many of my training liveries - a major component of my income was then gone. It is much better today that amateur and professional riders compete together.

Ferro

The Horse

Above *Ferro and Coby at home in the relaxed atmosphere of Stables van Baalen*
Opposite *Coby and Ferro riding the Grand Prix Team Test at the Australian Olympics 2000 where they placed 3rd individually and won the Team Silver medal*

A day in the life

Ferro was known as the 'Black Pearl' of the KWPN. He was a beautiful black stallion with a white star and blaze and three white socks. He started his competitive career as a show jumper but many people commented that his movements were so good he may make an even better dressage horse. So when Ferro was turning seven he arrived at Dressage Van Baalen stables to begin his cross training. Although Ferro was trained to Prix St Georges and showed great talent for the more advanced movements, we had to start at the beginning with him as he was a peculiar combination of being hotly spirited yet not listening to the aids. Once he learned the half-halts, the rhythm came and he found collection much easier, as he demonstrated many times in his piaffe and passage tours.

At home Ferro was the boss. He was very distracted by mares and would get very excited if one walked past his stable. Initially he was not so interested in people, but early on in our relationship we made a connection and he was very fixated on my groom, myself and, of course, Johann. He then became more personable and dependent on us and slowly became interested in people, showing a softer side to his character. But it took a long time to win his trust. When he arrived we had a special groom assigned to him who would spend the whole day just with him. She would sit with a bucket of feed and feed him by hand, patting his head and stroking his ears until, almost a year later, he became used to it and would let us do everything to him. However, he would only let people he knew well so close to him. Eventually he allowed us to spoil him with treats which he needed and enjoyed. Everyday Ferro would have his breakfast at 5:15 in the morning after which he would be hand walked before his covering duties began. He would be returned to his stable for hay and a rest before being ridden. In the afternoon he would be walked again and then hand grazed. To avoid the risk of him injuring himself in the field, as he was an approved stallion and did not belong to us, he was always hand grazed. Ferro had the same groom, Irene, the entire time he was with us.

Ferro's character and physical strength made dressage easy for him but as a breeding stallion, and he was in

Ferro's Competition Highlights

1998 Team Silver 6th Individually World Equestrian Games Rome, 3rd Dutch Championships in Nijmegen.

1999 Team Silver European Championships in Arnhem, 2nd Dutch Championships in Nijmegen, 1st CDI-W Berlin.

2000 Team Silver 5th Individually at Sydney Olympics, 2nd World Cup Final in Den Bosch, 1st World Cup Qualifier in Neumunster, 2nd Dutch Championships in Nijmegen.

2002 Team 5th at World Equestrian Games in Jerez Spain, Team Silver 4th Individually at CHIO Aachen, 2nd Dutch Championships in Nijmegen.

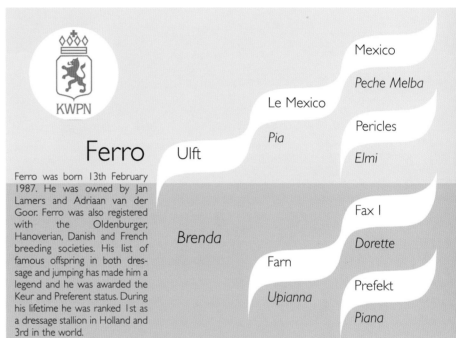

Ferro

Ferro was born 13th February 1987. He was owned by Jan Lamers and Adriaan van der Goor. Ferro was also registered with the Oldenburger, Hanoverian, Danish and French breeding societies. His list of famous offspring in both dressage and jumping has made him a legend and he was awarded the Keur and Preferent status. During his lifetime he was ranked 1st as a dressage stallion in Holland and 3rd in the world.

KWPN

Ulft — Le Mexico — Mexico
Peche Melba
Pia — Pericles
Elmi

Brenda — Farn — Fax I
Dorette
Upianna — Prefekt
Piana

great demand, he could be distracted easily during the busy breeding season. It was unfortunate that Ferro was injured after the Sydney Olympics in 2000. It was an injury that took almost two years to heal. But during an attempted comeback in 2002, the same injury was still present, so his owners decided to retire him from competitive life and concentrate on his breeding potential. In February 2005, Ferro was once again the focus of attention at the KWPN Stallion Licensing Show. Many of his licensed offspring were also present. Two weeks later, Ferro was found in the stable suffering from colic. Despite the best veterinary help which came to his aid immediately, there was nothing they could do to save him and Ferro was humanely put to sleep. During his life time he produced outstanding offspring and is still considered to be one of the foundation sires of the KWPN. He was ranked No.1 dressage stallion in the Netherlands and was ranked No. 3 in the world for all disciplines. Ferro, as an international Grand Prix horse was amazing, Ferro, as a breeding stallion is a legend.

Ferro's breeding record

Olympic Ferro was the highest placed KWPN (Royal Warmblood Studbook of the Netherlands) dressage stallion in Holland during his lifetime. In 2000, nine Ferro stallions made it through to the second stallion examination held in Ermelo, Holland. Out of the six stallions that were finally approved, two were sons of Ferro - Paddox and Pyriet. In previous years the KWPN had approved four sons of Ferro - Kennedy, Metall, Negro, and Osmium. The British Equestrian Society has approved two sons - Jazz Dancer and Lorenzo.

In 2001 at Den Bosch, Ferro had nine sons competing for approval and two were approved in the finals - Rousseau and Rhodium. During the auction that followed one of Ferro's sons, Rambo, was sold for 300,000 guilders to the US based Hilltop Farm. That same year Ferro also had an American-bred son going into the Oldenburg approval in Germany. Ferro's offspring do extremely well both in dressage and jumping.

In 2002 eleven Ferro sons were appointed for the second stallion examination held in 's Hertogenbosch. This was, at the time, the highest number of young stallions from the same sire which have made it through to the second round in any one year.

With these achievements it is no wonder that Ferro was ranked the number one stallion in the Netherlands and ranked in the top five of the world's best breeding stallions. Although Ferro's life ended unexpectedly his progeny can be seen competing and breeding successfully throughout the world today.

Coby and Ferro
Competing at Champion Gelderland in Arnhem, Netherlands. In this competition Ferro placed 1st in the Grand Prix against a very large field and 1st in the Grand Prix Special

Canter Half-Pass

Monica Theodorescu and Whisper

The horse should adopt a uniform bend into the direction in which he is moving, with his body becoming almost parallel to the long side of the arena, although the forehand should be fractionally in advance of the hindquarters. Each canter stride should 'spring' effortlessly forwards and sideways, following exactly the prescribed line. The horse is looking into the direction in which he is moving. He should maintain the same cadence and balance throughout the whole movement. In order to develop the ease and grace of the movement, it is of great importance, not only that the horse is correctly bent, but that this bend is soft, compliant and completely free from resistance, thereby allowing full impulsion to flow easily through the whole body.

Here we see one of the World's most classically trained and talented riders, Monica Theodorescu, performing the canter half-pass with her rising star, Whisper. This pair add a dimension of lightness and grace that is rare to see in modern day sport. Monica has a way of producing one Grand Prix horse after the next that makes everything they do appear poised and effortless, and in this picture, Whisper is no exception.

The lightness, ease and fluency of this movement is very easy on the eye - such a pleasure to watch. Whisper is perfectly positioned in this canter half-pass with his shoulders being fractionally in advance of his hindquarters, and his clear, uniform bend into the direction he is moving, appears extremely soft and compliant without being exaggerated or forced in any way. He is reaching into the movement with a confident ground covering stride. Although, for perfection, he could be a little higher at the poll. Whisper's balance and clarity of rhythm (note the diagonal left fore and right hind touching the ground at exactly the same moment) demonstrate some of the ideals one looks for.

Monica's stylish riding, with her characteristic poise and grace, gives her the appearance of being 'as one' with her horse. Perfectly balanced in the saddle, she is able to allow her horse to move effortlessly underneath her as if he is performing this beautiful canter half-pass

of his own accord. Monica's hands are level and are keeping a steady light contact which Whisper has accepted confidently. Monica is a very experienced rider having benefited from training with her late father, the famous George Theodorescu. Their training practices are all based on the traditional classical system of riding. The horses Monica has competed successfully at Grand Prix level for her country have been very different types but she has managed to bring their mental and athletic qualities to the fore by applying this system of training.

Although this is only a snapshot of Whisper, having judged this combination on many occasions, I have seen him float from one transition to the next without tension or resistance but full of impulsion and harmony responding to Monica's almost invisible commands. He is not exaggerated in his movements but the ease and fluency of every step he takes has been highlighted by Monica's excellent training. Whisper is still relatively young in terms of being an 'International Grand Prix horse but he has already established himself as one of the top ten international competitors. There is no doubt that as he matures and becomes stronger physically and mentally, his Grand Prix performances will develop even further. Monica and Whisper have a bright future together, but importantly he is a testament to the good training he has received.

George Theodorescu

The Trainer

Above *The late George Theodorescu watching his daughter ride. George always claimed the best example of his classical training methods is his daughter, Monica*
Right *George and Whisper no doubt discussing the strategy for the next Grand Prix*

Training Monica and Whisper

My father was taught how to handle and ride horses initially by his grandfather in Romania who instilled the belief that the only way to train a horse is to first become friends so that it is not frightened of you. To achieve this takes time, great patience and love - there are no short-cuts - there is no place for incorrect use of whips and spurs to punish a horse. When he was 31, he escaped from Romania to Germany as a political refugee. It was in Germany that he continued his training in classical dressage. So strong were his beliefs in the classical system that he resigned from the prestigious International Dressage Trainers' Club in 2007 stating that 'all concepts' of 'true' dressage art are being mixed by the modern trainers. Despite being a certified lawyer, he spent his entire life devoted to the training of horses.

When training Whisper, since we had had him as a four year old, we could bring him on totally with our own methods, as there were no bad habits to correct. Whisper is such a talented horse in that he had a supremely natural rhythm and regularity in his paces. We believe in and train for self-carriage. Although I started to ride him when he was four and a half, we did not start lunge work with him using the top check until he was seven. Every horse is different and the training must be adjusted to suit each horse. When one watches horses in the field they dance through their paces to show off in front of other horses. When we ride them we want to allow and encourage the horse to maintain this 'dance' in their paces - never to cause them to lose this desire. The horse must always feel that he can go forward so the reins must not be blocking him - pulling him back. The rider must constantly be thinking 'up-hill' into light hands. The half-halt that we employ teaches and encourages this way of thinking in the horse. The horse must be constantly praised during his work not just at the end. Balance is the essential element for both horse and rider. A good riding position is essential to good balance and you have to

My Story

1925 George was born in Bucharest, Romania.

1956 After competing in the Swedish Olympics for Romania George then fled to Germany as a political refugee.

1959 Although qualified to practice law in Germany his passion still remains with horses.

1978 The family move into Gestüt Lindenhof - Lime Tree Stud.

1991 Voted dressage trainer of the year by the International Dressage Trainers Association, George resigns from the organisation in 2007.

1996 George receives the German Golden Rider's Cross to honour his achievements in dressage.

2005 George receives the title of German Riding Master.

be fit to achieve this. For the horse, our method of lunging with the check rein encourages young horses to take weight behind, becoming lighter on the front, so they can balance more naturally, as it is the hind legs that produce the power. The rider must never pull the horse back to achieve the contact but rather the horse must go forward into the contact. In this way the horse will move with his shoulders up and his head in front of the vertical, which is how they would move out in the field. By doing lots of circles and serpentines you are asking the horse to bend and step under with his inside hind leg naturally. At home we do lots of training in this way - working on the basics, the way of going. Whisper knows the changes and half-passes so we will work on this only a few days before a show.

We never incorporate side-reins into our riding system, this method is forbidden to be practised on our farm. My father always said 'a riding master who uses side-reins is not a master at all'. There must be co-operation between horse and rider and side-reins do not encourage this.

I train everyday like my father has taught me and I rely on videos a lot to see how I am doing. Every now and then the German Team coach, comes over to see my routine and tell me what he thinks. But this is the only help I have now that my father is gone. I feel very comfortable in this situation.

At shows when I warm up, I like to be just with my horse. I prefer not to have people around. I am responsible for my horse and each show has its own rain, different arenas have their own problems and I have to use the warm-up to focus Whisper on me. When I enter the arena I have to be with my horse so that if there are 10 or 1000 people watching it doesn't matter because I am with my horse. To me this is what dressage is all about - to be totally focused on each other. I am not a nervous or panicky person. It is the way that I was brought up from the very beginning. My father would always say 'it is OK, just follow your line and your routine'.

Whisper
The Horse

A day in the life

I was first attracted to Whisper when I went to Ann-Kathrin Linsenhoff's stable to look at another horse. Whisper was very young at the time but already had an amazing walk with lovely supple cadence in his other movements. A month or so after this visit, a lorry arrived at our stable - Ann-Kathrin sent Whisper to us and he has remained with me ever since.

Whisper is still a young horse but he has achieved so much already. We started him off slowly, going to only a few competitions and spending more time training at home. He didn't really need to go to many shows for experience because the highly charged atmosphere which some shows generate did not affect him and for a young horse, this was quite exceptional. In his first Grand Prix Special in Dortmund, when he was only eight, not only did he win the class but he received three scores of 10's for different elements of the test. He is not the most flamboyant moving horse but his way of going is very correct and the judges award him for this. When he was only nine, Whisper was on the Silver medal German Team at the European Dressage Championships in Turin, Italy.

At home, Whisper is like a pet dog. He is a very sweet horse and would never have his ears back. Because of his kind nature, people are always giving him treats, which he loves.

My father had a belief that if you are spending so much money buying a good horse and spending so much of your time riding and training a horse, it would be stupid to just turn them out in a field in case they injured themselves. So instead Whisper is hacked out in the woods everyday for relaxation after his morning workout and then is grazed in-hand for hours by his groom. I used to have a lovely little grey mare called Fleur, who was also very talented and was competing at Grand Prix level but she broke her leg running free in the field, so perhaps my father was right - I won't take that chance with Whisper.

For all the time that Whisper has been with us at Gestüt Lindenhof, he has never had a bad day. The best part of my day is when I get to ride him. He is so much the product of how we have brought him up. He is so stable that to prepare him for the test is not an issue because he comes out as he has done day to day at home and does exactly the same when he is at shows. He is so young and there is so much more to come.

Whisper's Competition Highlights

2005 1st Prix St Georges 1st Intermediare at Bad Salzuflen.

2007 1st Grand Prix 9th Kur at CDI-W in Frankfurt, Team Silver, Individual 7th at European Championships in Italy, 1st Grand Prix Special at Dortmund, 1st Grand Prix Special Hagen, 2nd Grand Prix 1st Special Bad Salzuflen, Winner of the Otto Lorke prize for the most talented upcoming Grand Prix horse under 10yrs old in Germany.

2008 2nd CDI Grand Prix 3rd Special at Aachen, 3rd Grand Prix and Special at Bad Salzuflen.

2009 7th Grand Prix 6th Kur at World Cup Final in Las Vegas, 4th Grand Prix and Kur CDI-W 's Hertogenbosch, 3rd Grand Prix and Kur CDI-W Neumunster.

Whisper

Whisper is a beautiful Baden Wurttemberger chestnut gelding born in 1998 in Wurttemberger Germany. His breeder was Lothar Wanner from Wangen. Whisper was purchased by Ann-Kathrin Linsenhoff as a foal but was given to Monica by Ann-Kathrin to ride as a four year old.

Welt Hit	Weltmeyer	World Cup I
		Anka
	Cileste	Hill Hawk
		Cilla II
Widney	Weltstar	Weltmeister
		Rodila
	Eszra	Elfenglanz
		Artistin

Opposite *Whisper leaving the arena in Aachen 2008 after completing another successful Grand Prix test*
Above *Whisper enjoying the kindness and attention while his rider does last minute preparations before entering the arena in Frankfurt. Monica and Whisper went on to win the Grand Prix on a score of 72.97%*
Left *Whisper executing an expressive extended trot in front of the judges. Whisper gains his points not so much from being flamboyant but by being 'correct' in his movements*

Monica and Whisper on their victory lap
At the CDI-World Cup Qualifier in Stockholm held in the Globe Arena, Monica and Whisper placed 6th in the Grand Prix Kur. This enabled them to become one of fourteen to qualify for the World Cup Finals held in Las Vegas 2009.

The FEI World Cup Finals are held each year in different locations around the world. During the year, horse and rider combinations compete in special qualifying classes held in their geographical regions. The top combinations from each region are invited to compete against the best in the world at the Finals. In Las Vegas, Monica and Whisper placed 7th in the Grand Prix and 6th in the Grand Prix Kur.

The Ericsson Globe
The national indoor arena in Stockholm is named after Sweden's telecommunications company and is currently the largest hemispherical building in the world. It opened in 1989 after taking over two years to build and can seat up to 16,000 spectators. Mainly used for ice hockey events it makes a beautiful venue for the World Cup Qualifier

Photo, left: *Monica and Whisper in an elegant trot half-pass at the European Championships*

Canter Pirouette

Laura Bechtolsheimer and Mistral Hojris

The pirouette is a circle executed on two tracks, with a radius equal to the length of the horse. During the pirouette the forefeet and the outside hind foot move round the inside hind foot, which forms the very centre of the circle and in a perfect situation should spring from the ground and return, virtually to the same spot. The horse should adopt a soft, submissive bend into the direction in which he is turning, remaining 'on the bit' with a light contact, maintaining a good cadence and the appearance of a clear canter rhythm, although the feet of the diagonal are not touching the ground absolutely simultaneously. The poll stays the highest point during the entire movement. The horse maintains his impulsion and never moves backwards or deviates sideways with the hindquarters. There is a visible lowering of the haunches, with the horse carrying a greater proportion of his body weight on his hindquarters. Six to eight canter strides are desired to demonstrate that the rider is in control of the turn.

Laura Bechtolsheimer and Mistral Hojris have recently made a huge impact on the world stage of International Dressage. This highly talented young lady has developed a partnership with the immensely powerful and athletic Mistral Hojris that have spectators and judges alike sitting on the edge of their seats.

At 's Hertogenbosch this year, while I was awarding this combination 10's for some of the final Piaffe Passage tour of the Grand Prix Special, my writer asked if I wished to add a comment to go alongside the 10's - the only word that sprang to mind was 'Wow!'

Since then, this sensational combination have gone from strength to strength earning a Team Silver medal and Individual Bronze medal for Great Britain at the European Championships in Windsor.

Here in this picture the pair are performing the Canter Pirouette - the ultimate in collection. This massively powerful horse is carrying virtually all of his body weight on his hindquarters during this phase of the canter stride without any apparent effort or stress, which is testament to the years of gymnastic training it has taken to develop the suppleness and muscle power which allows this most difficult of all canter exercises to be performed with such assured ease and fluency. The lowering of the hindquarters is clearly visible along with the lightness and mobility of the shoulders. His self carriage is evident with his neck in a natural position with poll being the highest part and the front line of his face just ahead of the vertical, whilst accepting an elastic contact with the bit.

He is positively, but without exaggeration, positioned into the direction in which he is turning with a soft compliant contact on the inside (right) rein, allowing the rider to take his forehand easily around his hindquarters with the, still soft, but controlling outside (left) rein. The rider's body position is perfectly balanced over the horse's centre of gravity with her outside (left) leg drawn slightly back in order to 'guard' the hindquarters from deviating to the outside of the turn. Laura's inside leg (not visible in this picture) will be quietly, but effectively, by the girth, maintaining the energy and activity of each canter stride.

Laura Bechtolsheimer

The Rider

Above Laura taking a break at the Beijing Olympics. This big horse statue was covered with the signatures from all of the equestrian athletes

Opposite, top Feeling good - Laura just accepted the Bronze medal for the Grand Prix Special at the European Championships along with Gold medalist Adeline Cornelissen on Parzival and Silver medallist Edward Gal on Moorlands Totilas

Opposite, right Laura and Mistral Hojris riding the Grand Prix in Beijing in the presence of the Olympic flame

My most memorable test

The competition in Neumunster in 2006 where Mistral Hojris, or Alf as we call him at home, and I rode the Intermediary II is my most memorable test. It was our first time at that level together and we were in total harmony. He was listening so intently to everything I was asking him and he executed every movement so effortlessly and willingly. It was this test that told me beyond a shadow of a doubt that he could do the Grand Prix and do it well. The feeling I got from this test put to rest the doubts I may have had from listening to those who tried to convince me that Alf was a bad choice. I didn't know before we had bought him that several professional riders had tried him but found him far too difficult. Alf had run off with big men through several arenas totally out of control. Many said to my father that Alf was dangerous and it was criminal for him to let me ride Alf. Perhaps if we had known these things about Alf before we bought him we may have thought otherwise. But we had time for Alf we didn't need to rush him and this test was Alf paying me back for all the hard work we put into him. The arena at Neumunster was positioned close to the audience, he was very nervous. We entered and halted at X. Alf took a really deep breath. All the way through the test I kept saying to myself this is great. I had tears in my eyes at the end. This test gave me confidence to keep going with him. We won the class on 70.78%. The next week we scored only 50% but I knew we still had lots of training to do. Alf showed me the week before he had the talent and desire to do it, only his brain was stopping him and that was something I could work on.

My Story

1985 I was born in Germany, but moved to England with my parents when I was one year old.

1999 The first time I competed for Great Britain was on the International Pony Squad and from there on the Junior, Young and Senior Squads.

2005 Douglas Dorsey and I won the National Championships, I was the youngest person to win this competition. The same year I was also the youngest person to represent my country at an international dressage competition.

2007 Alf and I achieved the highest score for a British rider at an international Grand Prix with a score of 75.33%. Graduated from Bristol University with an MSc in Politics and Philosophy.

2008 Selected to represent my country at the Bejing Olympics. Voted British Dressage Rider of the Year.

My daily routine

When I am not away competing, I could have up to seven horses to ride at home in Cirencester. I ride them all in the morning because they all come out again to do exercises in the day. I divide my afternoons between the yard and working for the website, *Horsehero.com*. We not only train our own horses but we have a small breeding operation as well. It is a wonderful experience teaching the youngsters that you have known from

My Competition Highlights

1997 1st National School Championships in eventing.

1999 Silver Team medal Pony European Championships on Foresters Gold.

2000 Silver Team medal Pony European Championships on Golden Dancer.

2004 2nd Team Test 1st Kur at CDIYR Addington UK on Winniza, 4th team test 2nd Kur CDIYR in Hagen GER, Bronze medal Young Rider European Championships on Douglas Dorsey.

2005 1st British National

Championships on Douglas Dorsey.

2006 1st B Final at World Cup Championships in Amsterdam, represented GB at World Equestrian Games in Aachen on Douglas Dorsey.

2007 10th Grand Prix 7th Kur at Stuttgart, 5th Grand Prix 3rd Kur at CDI Lingen, 6th Grand Prix 3rd Kur at CDIO Aachen on Douglas Dorsey.

2008 1st Grand Prix National Championships, 10th Grand Prix 7th Kur at CDI Stuttgart on Andretti H.

2009 4th Grand Prix 5th Kur at CDI Hagen on Andretti H.

birth and watching them develop into good riding horses. I also spend time on my own fitness which I feel is an essential part to being a good athlete - which a dressage rider must be. I have lots of friends who do not ride so when I am out with them I can switch off from the horse world as they have no idea what 73% means. When competing I wouldn't say I was a superstitious person but I do find I wear the same set of small pearl earrings. Before a competition I like to visualise the tests in detail several times so there are no surprises on the day. I watch a few tests with my father and take in his comments. Sometimes if time permits I will have a nap just before I put on my top hat and tails. When riding the actual test I see nothing but the 'dance floor'. I have complete tunnel vision, I am good at putting pressure on myself as I don't like to let people down but I also keep this pressure in perspective so it is positive and creative.

How my riding career began

I started riding when I was three on my parent's farm in Gloucestershire, England. Whenever they took the dog for a walk I would tack up my pony and go along with them. Initially I evented, jumped, hunted and did anything that required nerves and speed but when I was thirteen I discovered dressage with all of its perfection, skill, and concentration - I was hooked. It was a big help when starting out that my father was a Grand Prix rider. His advice was then and still is now vital to my success. Ian Woodhead, British pony squad trainer, taught me the basics. Markus Gribbe was with me during the big step up to Grand Prix. Klaus Balkenhol helps me now and it was with him and my father that my scores really started to rise. It doesn't always go right in dressage but I have a very supportive family who are the machinery behind what makes all of this possible.

Dr Wilfried Bechtolsheimer

The Trainer

Above *Dr. Bechtolsheimer smiling proudly having just watched his daughter ride another Grand Prix test good enough for 2nd place at Stuttgart. Dr. Bechtolsheimer believes 'If you are happy with your life you can do anything, being able to laugh makes the setbacks easier to get over. In dressage you can always see trainers and riders smiling but we can do with much more smiling.'*

My Story

1948 I was born in Germany.

1986 We move from Germany to England when the children are school age to make England our home.

1995 Six months after receiving British citizenship I am selected to represent my new country at the European Championships.

1992 My horse Giorgione is selected for Barcelona Olympics with Carl Hester riding.

2008 Laura competes on Mistral Hojris at the Beijing Olympics.

Training Laura and Mistral Hojris

I recognised not only talent in my daughter, Laura, when she was very young but also star quality. Laura has had set backs in her career like any rider has but it is her ability to bounce back that makes the difference. When her horse Placido, for instance, developed a tumour on his leg and she thought she would not be able to qualify for the GB Young Rider squad, I offered Laura my mare Winniza to ride and she clicked instantly with her. However shortly after this mare also ran into difficulties with a virus so Laura was again without a horse and now running out of time to qualify. I then offered Laura my Grand Prix horse Douglas Dorsey who can be strong and wilful. Laura was not keen on the idea initially but after only a few days training with him, she said to me that 'I had lost my horse' as she wasn't giving him back. This is why I find teaching my own daughter at this supreme level of dressage a joy - she never gives up, she looks at setbacks not as disappointments but as opportunities to try something else - something different. I think this is also what they call 'star quality' and she has it - it goes beyond talent and she has that too.

During our training sessions at home we work on every aspect of the horse and rider, Laura's position, Alf's way of going and the execution of the movements. Laura likes horses which are very big and have lots of motivation, and Alf is all of this. He may not always be the safest of rides for her but he is the sort of horse she has always clicked with so a lot of our time is spent learning to control Alf while not interfering with his big extravagant movement.

At a show we have a full training session two hours before Laura's test time and then twenty minutes before she and Alf are to enter the arena we come out to the practice arena just to relax Alf and loosen him up. At this point Alf needs very little motivation, he knows what is coming and our job is not to over excite him.

Laura is my only student as I am not a professional trainer. In the past I have trained Carl Hester and a few others but now all my attention is on Laura. My knowledge of riding stems primarily from the training I received from Harry Boldt, Herbert Rehbein and Sheila Wilcox, although an eventer Sheila greatly influenced my dressage. I believe strongly in the 'classical' approach to riding and being kind to the horse always comes first. It has been rewarding to train our horses ourselves in a kind way and to see them win because of how they have been trained. Judges can only see what is in the arena not the training at home - perhaps they need to be more aware of competitor's training practices. I have noticed at a number of competitions that there are many young A squad riders coming up through the ranks from Holland, Germany and Great Britian who have a solid grounding in the 'classical' way of training and this is good.

Left *Laura, her father and mother watching the competition warming up*
Middle, left *Laura and Alf leaving the arena having just completed the Grand Prix Special which won them the Bronze medal much to the delight of Team Captain Richard Davison*
Below, right *Dr. Bechtolsheimer checking the saddle is secure before Laura starts her training*
Below, left *Laura and Mistral Hojris competing at Olympia under the watchful eye of her parents. Laura derives great strength from the fact that her family are involved in her competitive career*

Mistral Hojris

The Horse

A day in the life

Mistral Hojris or 'Alf' as he is known at home is a big gentle giant. He was given the name Alf after a cartoon character who was a big orange fluffy alien. Alf is a very cuddly horse who likes nothing more than to have someone around to talk to him and pat him all day.

At home Alf has a pretty consistent routine. He is fed in the morning and then is ridden or trained by me. He

Above *Mistral Hojris, looking more like the big orange fluffy giant he was named after, is about to begin his Grand Prix test in the pouring rain at Rotterdam CDIO. Dressage horses have to perform their test at specified times regardless of the weather*
Right *Mistral Hojris and an appreciative Laura just completing their test in Stuttgart. Despite Alf's huge size and imposing presence he relies on Laura for confidence and security particularly in arenas filled to capacity with spectators*

is then washed down and dried by his groom Carole who looks after him at home and when we are away competing so she knows every hair on Alf's body. The washing is followed by an extensive grooming session which we believe is a reward for the horse and something they can look forward to. During this grooming we use a traditional technique called 'banging' or 'strapping'. This is where the groom takes a dry clean cloth and slaps it against the horses body at certain points (of which there are three)and then slides the cloth off. This is repeated about twenty times at each of the three points. My father was taught this method by Sheila Wilcox the famous British event rider. We are probably one of the very few stables left who still use this system of grooming but it has done Alf's sensitive physique a world of good keeping him toned and sound as the muscles tighten and relax throughout the slapping process.

Despite Alf's enormous size he is such a big baby and relies on me for confidence and security especially in the show ring. However, once he has completed his test and is feeling much more familiar with his environment his confidence bubbles over and he can become the world's biggest show-off and very difficult to handle. Most times at prize givings I have to ride his stable mate the reliable Douglas Dorsey who remains calm throughout all the applause, ribbons and loud music. Alf is very big and very strong so having lots of time to work with him keeps him relaxed and amenable. He is a lovable giant and I knew he was the one for me the instant my father showed him to me on a video. He hasn't disappointed and we have only just begun.

Mistral Hojris' Competition Highlights

2005 5th Young Riders Kur 4th Prix St Georges CDIYR Saumur, Bronze medal in the Kur Young Rider European Championships Barzago Italy.

2006 2nd Grand Prix Special at CHIO Aachen.

2007 Qualified for World Cup Final in Las Vegas, 13th Grand Prix European Championships in Turin Italy, 2nd Grand Prix 5th Kur World Cup Qualifier at Olympia, 8th Grand Prix 6th Special at Stuttgart German Masters, 1st Grand Prix 9th Kur CDI Hagen, 3rd Grand Prix 2nd Special at CDI Lingen.

2008 2nd Grand Prix Special Stuttgart, 5th Grand Prix Kur Rotterdam, 6th Grand Prix Special and Kur Hagen, represented GB at Bejing Olympics, 2nd Grand Prix Special Stuttgart, 2nd Grand Prix 4th Kur at Olympia UK.

2009 1st Grand Prix and Special CDI 's Hertogenbosch, 3rd Grand Prix 4th Kur CDI-W Neumunster, 1st Grand Prix and Special at CDI Hagen, 3rd Grand Prix and Kur at Hickstead CDIO, Team Silver, Individual Bronze 4th Kur at European Championships at Windsor.

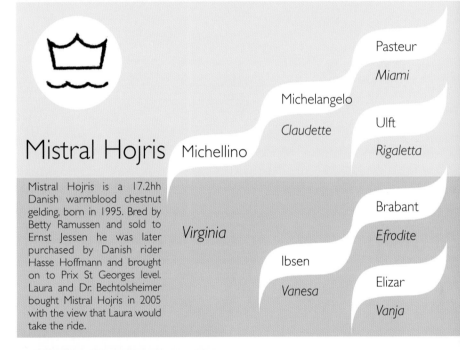

Mistral Hojris

Mistral Hojris is a 17.2hh Danish warmblood chestnut gelding, born in 1995. Bred by Betty Ramussen and sold to Ernst Jessen he was later purchased by Danish rider Hasse Hoffmann and brought on to Prix St Georges level. Laura and Dr. Bechtolsheimer bought Mistral Hojris in 2005 with the view that Laura would take the ride.

Michellino — Michelangelo — Pasteur / Miami

Michelangelo — Claudette — Ulft / Rigaletta

Virginia — Ibsen — Brabant / Efrodite

Vanesa — Elizar / Vanja

Left The comfortable stables provided for the British equestrian teams at the 2008 Hong Kong Olympics. They were temperature controlled to make it as comfortable for the equine athletes as possible

Concentration and focus are everything

When Laura and Mistral Hojris enter the arena Laura sees nothing but the 'dance floor'. The flags, the audience, the flowers at ring side are just a big blur when they are riding the test. The enormous amount of time and hard work riders must devote to training counts for nothing if they become distracted by the surroundings or allow the pressure of the moment to overwhelm them.

   Mistral Hojris is such a big horse but found many situations scary which in the early days could disrupt his test. Laura and her father took their time bringing him on slowly, building up his confidence at home so that now he is capable of producing near fault free tests regardless of what is happening around the arena. Together at the 2009 European Championships at Windsor they won the Team Silver medal in the Grand Prix and the Individual Bronze medal for the Grand Prix Special and placed 4th in the Grand Prix Kur.

Windsor Castle
Windsor Castle provided the picturesque background for the 2009 European Dressage Championships. The largest inhabited castle in the world it is the oldest castle in continuous occupation and is one of the principle residences of the British monarch, Queen Elizabeth II. Most of the Kings and Queens of Great Britain have had influence on its evolving construction. The parks surrounding the castle have been used many times to hold major equestrian events including eventing, carriage driving and show jumping

Flying Changes

Ulla Salzgeber and Rusty

The flying change of leg is executed during the period of suspension which follows the three beat sequence of the canter stride. Flying changes of leg can also be executed in series, at every fourth, third, second and every stride. The horse, even in series, remaining light, calm and straight with lively impulsion, maintaining the same rhythm and balance throughout the series concerned. In order to demonstrate the lightness, fluency and expression of the flying changes of leg in series, a lively impulsion must be maintained.

We have never before seen within the sport of dressage a combination capable of producing flying changes of this quality. Ulla Salzgeber and her 'horse of a lifetime', Rusty, will surely go down in history as one of the greatest partnerships of all time. From this lovely illustration, the immense power combined with such lightness and elasticity is easy for all to see. The perfect straightness and uphill balance of the horse is complemented by his enormous impulsion which is completely free from anxiety or tension. It is these qualities that allow them to produce such superb ground covering changes.

In both the two tempi and one tempi changes they consistently made the first change on virtually the first stride of the diagonal line and finished on the last stride, a rarity indeed but probably necessary if Rusty was to fit in all the required strides! Rusty seemed to put all of his energy into every generous stride he took, with his brilliant rider measuring every footfall so that the changes fitted exactly on the entire diagonal line.

For the rest of my days I will never forget what a privilege it was to sit at C during the Grand Prix at the Olympic Games in Athens and to be able to award the ultimate 10, not only for these fabulous flying changes, but also for Ulla's magnificent riding. Her perfect position in the saddle and the way in which she is able to influence her great partner, Rusty, is an example to all who aspire to reach the very top of the dressage sport.

Their presence together in the arena was commanding but elegant. Ulla's penchant for perfection in both her classical training techniques and showmanship were very evident when she and Rusty were competing. Both horse and rider seemed to melt into one.

To think that it was only by chance that this famous partnership ever came together in the first place. Ulla had decided to put more of her concentration into teaching her many students, rather than her competitive career when Rusty, from unknown heritage, arrived all the way from Latvia. He was only to be reschooled by Ulla before being sold on, but when Ulla sat on Rusty for the very first time she knew instantly that he was indeed something very special.

There is of course an element of 'good luck' when competing but Ulla and Rusty's success was based almost entirely on Ulla's superb training and riding ability. Rusty was not always the easiest of mounts as he could be wary of 'monsters' hiding in the decorations which surround the arena - producing tension which could have had devastating consequences on their final scores. Ulla's unwavering concentration and focus ensured that Rusty did not succumb to his fears. Her determined riding seemed to fill him with the confidence he needed to 'attack' the test and perform to his maximum. All of which was instrumental to them amassing an enviable collection of Gold medals.

Ulla Salzgeber

The Rider

My most memorable test

I had the ride of my life on Rusty at the European Championships at Hickstead in 2003. Due to recent press reports, I was angry and determined to show the world that Rusty and I did not need the help of outside influences to win medals. And win medals we did, Individual Gold, Team Gold and Individual Open Gold - no one could touch us. I did not give Rusty the chance to misbehave, as sometimes he will spook at the flowers, I told him he was going to stay with me during the entire tests and he did.

My daily routine

Although horses have always played a major part in my life, I have found time to focus on many other activities as well. I studied law, I was and still am a model for an equestrian clothing company and a mail order catalogue, I run my busy farm in Bad Worishofen. Today one of the greatest satisfactions in my life is training riders and horses. My students are from every corner of the globe so I am frequently travelling to give clinics and attend competitions as a coach. I generally like to visit the same group of riders each time so I have the pleasure of seeing them improve and achieve their goals. Each of my students is taught in exactly the same way but each horse is schooled differently. All the mistakes made by the horse are a result of either the rider's concentration lapsing or a fault in the rider's position. I put great emphasis on the rider's mental strength - to be able to visualize the perfect movements and to harmonize with the horse to create these perfect movements. The results do not happen overnight but are achieved through continuous systematic classical

Above *Ulla Salzgeber showing off her double gold medals at the 2003 European Championships at Hickstead England. Ulla and Rusty went on to win a third Gold medal, the Individual Open Gold medal. As Ulla declared 'no one could touch us'*

Right *Ulla and Rusty in a dramatic ground covering trot half-pass at Aachen. One of Ulla and Ernst's worries when a movement required a specific number of strides was that Rusty might not be able to fit them all in due to the immense length of his strides*

My Story

1958 Born 5th August in Oberhausen, Rheinland, Germany.

1968 My first introduction to riding was learning to vault on horseback.

1977 After years of hard work I became a member of the Junior/ Young Rider 'C' Team.

1979 In recognition of my successes in dressage I was presented with a gold 'German Riding Insignia'.

2005 My competitive journey with Rusty ended and he was retired. Thinking I will never have a horse like this again I once again turned to my passion - teaching.

2007 Now the rider of two very promising young horses Wakana and Herzruf's Erbe I begin to compete again.

training with the rider concentrated on their goal. The rider must develop harmonious control and take responsibility for all that happens between them and their horse.

Before Rusty came into my life I had given up international competitions to focus on teaching. But Rusty changed all of that. I realised what talent he had and tried once again to make the National squad - succeeding this time. When Rusty retired, I returned to my love - teaching. However, I now have a few stunning young horses which may insist I take up international competitions once again.

Ulla's Competition Highlights

1973 Team Gold at Junior European Championships in Aachen.

1975 Team Gold Junior European Championships in Fontainbleau.

1977 Team Gold 4th Individual at Young Rider European Championships in Leverkusen Germany.

1998 3rd Grand Prix and 2nd Kur in Stuttgart on Wallstreet.

1999 1st Grand Prix and 2nd Kur in Stuttgart on Wallstreet.

2001 1st Grand Prix and Kur at Neumunster on Wallstreet.

2003 1st Grand Prix and Kur at Stuttgart on Wallstreet, 1st Grand Prix and Special in Aachen on Wallstreet.

2008 1st Grand Prix and Kur in Verden on Herzruf's Erbe.

2009 1st Grand Prix at CDI Stadl Paura on Herzruf's Erbe. Silver medal Nations Cup CHIO Aachen on Herzuf's Erbe, 8th CDI Grand Prix at Aachen, 1st Grand Prix at Heroldsberg on Wakana.

How my riding career began

I first started riding as a child when my brother and I would go on holiday, our treat was to have riding lessons at the local club. However it was not dressage that I practiced first but Vaulting! My first two dressage horses, Lutz and Glenfiddich, I trained myself to Grand Prix level. We participated on all of the German international squads for over a decade, but it was with Rusty that I reached the top and realised my dream.

I was educated at home and my parents insisted on the best teachers - Harry Boldt, Willi Schultheiss and General Albert Stecken. It was General Albert Stecken that was responsible for my love of training. But my determination to be the best has been my greatest teacher. About 25 years ago, I was watching Herbert Rehbein riding at a local show in Bavaria. I told myself, 'this is how I want to sit' and through hard work, I modelled my own position after him. I try to teach this position to all of my students. Many people have commented on my power of concentration. This ability came about after an unfortunate experience when I was riding my horse, Glenfiddich, in an important selection competition in Germany. During the test, 20 or 30 lorry horns suddenly sounded in protest to something. My horse did not flinch but, for a moment, I looked up, lost my way and became angry and anxious. The remainder of the test did not go well - it was a disaster and I told myself that will never happen again. The test was recorded so I could clearly see my break in concentration and how it affected my test. Now when I enter the arena I remain totally focused, if everything around me explodes, then it explodes, and I continue with my test because I do not hear it.

Above *Ernst Hoyos, one of the most respected and knowledgeable dressage trainers today. Ernst gave up the competitive side of his career because he enjoys teaching horses and riders much more*
Opposite *Ernst Hoyos at the Spanish Riding School where he spent the majority of his life learning and training*
Opposite, Top *Ulla and Ernst warming up before the Grand Prix at Aachen 2009. Ernst has been Ulla's trainer for over twelve years and although Rusty is retired Ulla has found inspiration in a new horse, that has motivated her to compete once again*
Opposite, Right *Ulla and Ernst relaxing after hectic training sessions but no doubt discussing horses*

Ernst Hoyos
The Trainer

Training Ulla and Rusty

When Ulla first got Rusty, she attended local shows with him at the Prix St Georges level and he was winning everything. Soon people were coming to her saying Rusty was one of the best horses in Germany and if he was more educated they could be on the National team. Johann Hinnemann was the National coach at the time, along with Klaus Balkenhol, so Ulla took Rusty to him for his assessment. Jo was instantly amazed and they started to work together. Being National coach meant Jo was very busy and Ulla could not train as often as was necessary. Jo and I had been friends for many years and, since I lived much closer to Ulla than he did, he suggested that I help her. We did not hit it off immediately but now we do - there is a lot of respect between us and usually we train together every 14 days.

I could see instantly that Rusty had great potential and a huge personality. He was very big and could be difficult to hold in hand when he became afraid, which was frequent, as he often thought there were monsters in the flower beds. Initially he had difficulty with collection in some of the movements because of his big mechanical physique. Piaffe was probably the movement he disliked most and I know in the last competition he and Ulla would ever ride together, she promised him he would never have to do another piaffe for the rest of his life. Rusty had gigantic paces unlike any other horse I knew at that time. So big were his paces we were concerned that the arena would be too short for him to fit in the 15 one time changes or the nine, two time changes that were required in the Grand Prix tests - he would often use the entire diagonal line when performing the two tempi, in comparison to the majority of horses who could fit the requirements into 40 metres. From the extended trot to the half-passes, his paces were explosive and the transitions seamless. Rusty's walk rhythm in the early years also took some work on Ulla's part. She would do her daily training on him in the morning and then in the afternoon she would spend time just on his walk. Ulla's patient teaching has paid off for both of them.

It was not always possible for me to travel to competitions with Ulla. At the bigger events that I did attend, we would work on balance between horse and rider and harmony, which can be difficult for a rider if they are under pressure, particularly in Germany where there is keen competition to make the National squads.

I used to compete on my own horses when I lived in Austria, while I was still at the Spanish Riding School. At the same time, I had several students I taught in the evenings. It all became too much to teach and then compete against my students, so sadly I gave up the competing. I now own 4 or 5 horses at any one time that I use for my students to train on.

When I left the Spanish Riding School I moved to Germany to work because competitive dressage is much more interesting there. The number of students I teach has grown to 30 or 40 and they include Olympic candidates to the lower levels of dressage. My goal is always to produce another world-class champion horse and rider.

It was fascinating for me to grow up at home with between 60 to 80 horses of all types and breeds. I wanted to learn more and so I spent 29 years at the Spanish Riding School. There were good teachers but there were also trainers who could not explain so well how to do things. Instead you could understand by watching. I learned so much from watching and stealing tips from lots of very good riders. I strongly believe every rider has to find their own way.

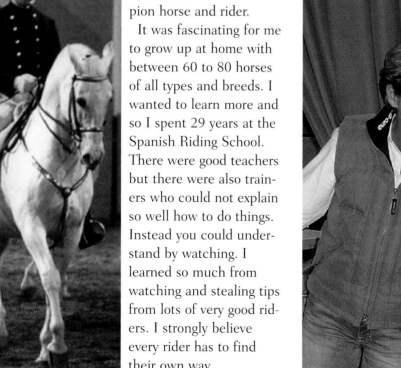

Above *Ulla and Rusty on their victory lap of honour at the European Championships at Hickstead 2003*
Opposite, Top *Ulla and Rusty smile for the crowd for the last time at Rusty's retirement party in Balve, Germany*
Opposite, bottom *Rusty with his best friend Motte enjoying a happy relaxing retirement in his field. Rusty's new home is not far from Ulla so she can visit him often*

Rusty
The Horse

A day in the life

Rusty's life, before he met me, was very different to most dressage horses who compete at his level. He was raced around fields bareback, went swimming, and was jumped on a regular basis. When he came to our barn as one of a group of horses to be trained and sold, he was a very thin six year old with his dressage talents well concealed. Once I saw him trot I knew he was something very special - two weeks later we won our first Prix St Georges. I bought Rusty immediately, with a view of achieving one of my dreams, Olympic Gold - he has not let me down. Just before Rusty arrived at our stables, I had decided to give up competing and to focus more on training riders and horses - little did I know that one of my first commissions would be Rusty, who immediately made me change course and return to international competitions.

Rusty was a fabulous Grand Prix horse with the most amazing ground covering strides but it will be his emotional Kur that he will be remembered for most. The music we choose for this kur, Carmina Burana by Carl Orff, suited his power and energy perfectly. Many people have told us they had goosebumps or felt close to tears watching this performance. Rusty himself seemed to like the music and would rise to the occasion when it started to play. In one of his tests at a CHIO, his score consisted of four '10s', five '9.5s' for the collective marks and many, many '9s' throughout the test. He knew perfectly well the standing ovations we received were really for him.

Behind the scenes Rusty initially took some managing. He was fine in the lorry as long as it was moving but if we were delayed in traffic, he would start to piaffe and get hot and agitated. At shows he could never be left for more than ten minutes before he would start running around his stable, trying to jump over the door. You could not even tie him up - he would break the halter and lead rope. One time he reared up in his stable and hung his front legs over a pipe cutting through a vein. There was blood everywhere. In two weeks,

Rusty's Competition Highlights

1998 3rd Grand Prix Special and Kur at Aachen, Team Gold and Individual Bronze at World Equestrian Games in Rome, 2nd Grand Prix at Stuttgart.

1999 2nd Grand Prix Stuttgart, 2nd Grand Prix Special, 3rd Kur in Aachen, Team Gold and Individual Silver at European Championships in Arnhem.

2000 1st Grand Prix and Kur in Stuttgart, Team Gold, 8th Grand Prix Special, Individual Bronze at Sydney Olympics.

2001 1st Grand Prix Stuttgart, 1st Grand Prix and Kur at Dusseldorf, Team Gold and Individual Gold at European Championships in Verden, 1st World Cup Final in Aarhus.

2002 1st World Cup Final in 's Hertogenbosch, Team Gold, Individual Bronze WEG in Jerez, 1st Grand Prix and Kur in Berlin.

2003 Team Gold and Individual Gold European Championships at Hickstead, German Dressage Champions, Team and Individual Gold in Aachen.

2004 Team Gold CHIO Aachen, Team Gold, Individual Silver, 1st Special, 2nd Kur at Athens Olympics - Rusty retires from competitions.

Rusty

Rusty is a chestnut gelding born April 1988 on the Stud farm Burtnieki in Latvia. He is 3/4 Hanoverian and his original name was Rotors. When Rusty was two he was sold to Belarus. In 1994 he was sent to Ulla's yard by Alexander Moksel for training with the view to being sold. Only two weeks later, after winning his first Prix St Georges, Ulla bought Rusty so that she may achieve her goal of participating in the Olympics. Rusty has remained with Ulla throughout his competitive career and now into his retirement.

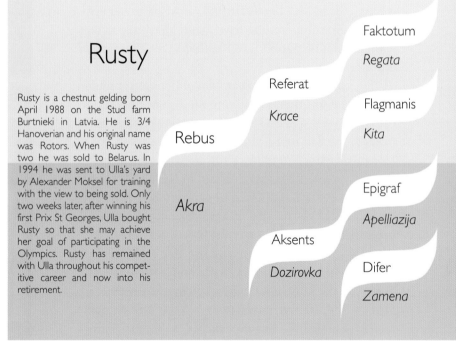

Rebus
— Referat
— — Faktotum
— — Regata
— Krace
— — Flagmanis
— — Kita

Akra
— Aksents
— — Epigraf
— — Apelliazija
— Dozirovka
— — Difer
— — Zamena

much to our vets amazement, Rusty was back in the competition arena - he never took a lame step - such was the stuff this tough horse was made of.

Over the years Rusty did become more relaxed but he always preferred to have the company of people. However, even today you have to be careful when changing his rugs or he will give you a little nip. Now in his retirement, he goes out in his field every day with his little pony friend Motte. Although she is only 8 hands high, she bosses him around and he loves it. They live in a retirement home where all their needs are met and he gets the attention that he deserves. I have been very fortunate to have had Rusty in my life.

Nerves of steel

Ulla Salzgeber and Rusty wowing the judges in extended trot at Aachen. Rusty had the most extravagant ground covering strides particularly in trot and canter. There was great concern that he would not be able to fit in both canter pirouettes when on the centre line as he had to include a specific number of flying changes in between. Rusty would often use the entire diagonal line when performing the two tempi in comparison to the majority of horses who could fit the requirements in to 40 metres. From the extended trot to the half-passes his paces were explosive and the transitions seamless.

The concentration of the rider is an absolute necessity when competing to win. Ulla claims that some journalists have described her as having 'ice water' in her veins. But Ulla says 'you have to have mental fortitude to cope with and not be put off by all mishaps that can happen' during a test.

Ulla's most public demonstration of her concentration and mental fortitude was during the Grand Prix Kur at the Sydney Olympics. The CD player broke halfway through the Kur just at the beginning of her walk tour. Horse and rider had to leave the arena, while the officials tried to sort out the problem. In the meantime the next competitor was allowed to perform their test using a backup CD player. Ulla, in the warm up arena, had to keep sharp and ready to go. The judges said the fault was a result of the machine and not Ulla's CD so they were allowed to re-enter the arena and resume the Kur at exactly the same place where the music stopped. Despite this massive interruption to their routine, they managed to win the Bronze medal.

Ground covering paces
Ulla and Rusty executing another ground covering extended trot in the Grand Prix at the CHIO Aachen in 2003. In this class they placed 1st. on a score of 75.88% which contributed to the German Team winning the Gold medal in the Nations' Cup

Extended Canter

Anky van Grunsven and Salinero

In the extended canter, the horse covers as much ground as possible. Maintaining the same tempo as the collected canter, he lengthens his strides to the utmost, as a result of great impulsion from the hindquarters, without losing any of his calmness, lightness or straightness. The rider allows the horse, while remaining 'on the bit', to lengthen his frame in relation to his strides. The cadence, straightness and balance during the transitions from both collected canter to extended canter and extended canter to collected canter should be maintained.

The legendary 'multi medallist', Anky van Grunsven, illustrated here with her double Olympic Gold medal winner, Salinero, during the extended canter. This illustration, shows quite a breathtaking example of impulsion at its utmost. Both horse and rider appear to be in perfect balance and in complete harmony with one another.

The power and energy that Salinero demonstrates during this period of the canter sequence is all the more impressive because of the calmness and confidence that he exudes through his magnificent expression. Of course the ability to perform this maximum extension in the canter is only possible when the collection of the horse has truly developed, which in Salinero's case it certainly has. This collection enables Anky to ask her horse to spring effortlessly upwards and forwards through the air in the extended strides which cover an enormous amount of ground with each bound of the canter, without in any way speeding up the tempo or change in the rhythm.

Equally impressive is Salinero's ability to return from this maximum extension to the collected canter again within very few strides. This demonstrates Salinero's understanding and quick reaction to the subtle, but effective, half halts given by his rider. In the end, it is the horse's ability to expand and contract both within the strides and the frame like a concertina, without any alteration of rhythm or loss of balance or straightness, tension free that convinces one of the true excellence of the whole dressage exercise.

I recall seeing Anky at the Athens Olympic Games in 2004, on a young Salinero where, to everyone's surprise, they took the Gold medal, the rhythm and harmony between the two was already well established and the experienced Anky guided her partner through the movements to victory.

Having had the undoubted honour of judging Anky van Grunsven on many occasions and on many of her horses over the years, I often think how fortunate we are in the dressage world to have this incredible rider in our midst. Anky, almost single handed, has in particular brought the Kur (the undoubted shop window of the sport) to a level that had not been dreamed of before. It has reached beyond the converted enthusiasts to an expanded spectator base who appreciate quality performing arts from any sphere as well as inspiring a whole generation of young hopefuls.

To my mind, especially when I think of her glorious partnership with Bonfire, they were surely the 'Torvill and Dean' of dressage, and then to follow this act with a second partner equally as successful says much for Anky's ability to firstly choose the right partner and then to patiently and systematically bring their abilities and talent to fruition.

Anky van Grunsven

The Rider

My most memorable test

My most memorable test was at the Athens Olympics in 2004. After a difficult year in 2003 - where I lost my father and broke my leg - it was very nice to win these Olympics. It was made more special because no one thought I would be the champion. With Salinero so young and relatively inexperienced, I was not the favourite as I had been when I won the Individual Gold medal on Bonfire at the 2000 Sydney Olympics in Australia. Salinero was going well but we still had a few years of training to go before perfection set in to win Olympic Gold medals. No one was more surprised than I at our success at these Olympics and I was also four months pregnant with my first child, Yannick Janssen. Salinero went so well Sjef thought he deserved to win and to think that there was still so much more to come.

My daily routine

My horses are fed early in the morning and I will normally come down to the stables to start riding about 9am. I used to ride from 8am to 8pm but now I ride only 5 horses each day which has reduced my riding time to include only my most promising horses such as I.P.S. Salinero and I.P.S. Painted Black. I have a family now and I want to spend time with my two children and my clothing business which is going well and needs more of my attention. I have also slimmed down my teaching time, to include only my best and most motivated students.

Above *Anky and 'that' famous smile. She and Salinero have just finished the Grand Prix Kur at CDIO Rotterdam 2008 to take first place*
Right *Winning the World Cup Final at 's Hertogenbosch against very stiff competition. Anky's ability to produce high scoring Kurs has left her and her equine partners in first place on many occasions*

My Story

1968 I was born on January 2nd 1968 in Erp, Netherlands.

1988 The Olympics in Seoul was my first Olympics, I rode Prisco, whom I had ridden since I was twelve.

2000 I was awarded the millenium title of honour 'Rider of the Century'.

2001/02 Bonfire retired from an illustrious competition career.

2004 My first child, Yannick Janssen was born, I received the Sport Star Award.

2005 Sjef, my trainer, and I were married by an Elvis Presley look-a-like in Las Vegas.

2007 I was declared the Netherlands top sports female earner. My daughter, Ava Eden was born.

How my riding career began

I have always had horses around me when I was growing up, as my older brothers rode and trained jumping horses in their spare time. I had a pony when I was six but Prisco was my first horse which my father bought for me when I was 12. He was supposed to be a jumping horse but he was quite lively so I practised dressage with him to give me more control. As it turned out he did not like to jump anyway so we continued with dressage. I went to my first Olympic games in 1988 on Prisco. Since then I have been to five other Olympics on Bonfire and Salinero. Bonfire was a great horse which I bought as a two and a half year old. He was very nervous and scared of everything but found all of the advanced movements so easy, like the passage and piaffe. It was the walk he found most difficult. Salinero followed on from Bonfire.

Although Sjef's and my training methods have certainly brought the best out in all of my horses, I think my most powerful weapon in competitions has always been my mental attitude. The ability to cope with the stress of getting to the top and then staying there when others do not want you to win is something I continually work on to improve. A long time ago I made the decision that I would ride for my own expectations and pleasure. I would not work this hard just to win because I do not control the decisions of the judges but I do have control over my own expectations and enjoyment when I ride.

Dressage has certainly become more popular since I started riding. Who would have thought school children would find a Grand Prix rider more popular than a soccer star? I am pleased that I have been able to promote the sport and encourage more people to take up dressage. Over the past decade, membership in the Dutch Equestrian Federation has grown over 40 per cent and hopefully it will continue to grow.

People have asked me how I stay motivated after having two wonderful horses but I just think riding is the most fun there is. I like to compete because I want to improve and at a show that is more difficult to do than at home.

Recently I have been taking Western reining lessons on a quarter horse, which I really enjoy. I am now looking for a suitable reining horse for myself. Who knows?, perhaps we will be good enough to compete in two disciplines at the next World Equestrian Games.

My Competition Highlights

1988 Team 5th at Seoul Olympics on Prisco.

1990 Dutch National Stallion Champion on Olympic Cocktail, Dutch National Champion on Prisco.

1991 Dutch National Champion on Bonfire.

1992 Team Silver, 4th Individual at Barcelona Olympics, Dutch National Champion on Bonfire, 1st World Cup Qualifier at Goodwood on Olympic Cocktail.

1993 Dutch National Champion on Bonfire.

1994 2nd Team, 1st Kur at WEG in The Hague, Dutch National Champion on Bonfire.

1995 1st World Cup Final in Los Angeles, 2nd Individual and Team at European Championships at Mondorf, Dutch National Champion on Bonfire.

1996 1st World Cup Final in Gothenburg, Team Silver and Individual Silver at Atlanta Olympics, Dutch National Champion on Bonfire.

1997 1st World Cup Final in 's Hertogenbosch, 2nd Individual and Team at European Championships at Verden, Dutch National Champion on Bonfire.

1998 Dutch National Champion, 2nd World Cup Final Gothenberg, 2nd Team, 1st Grand Prix Special at WEG in Rome on Bonfire.

1999 1st World Cup Final in Dortmund, 1st Individual, 2nd Team European Championships at Arnhem, Netherlands on Bonfire.

2000 1st World Cup Final in 's Hertogenbosch, Team Silver and Individual Gold medal at the Sydney Olympics, Dutch National Champion on Bonfire.

2003 2nd World Championships for Young Horses on I.P.S. Painted Black.

2008 2nd Grand Prix and Kur CDI-W Stockholm, 2nd Grand Prix and Kur CDI-W Mechelen, 1st Grand Prix Dutch Indoor Championships on I.P.S. Painted Black.

2009 2nd Grand Prix, 1st Kur CDI-W Amsterdam, 3rd World Cup Final in Las Vegas on I.P.S. Painted Black.

Sjef Janssen
The Trainer

Training Anky and Salinero

My wife Anky and I met in 1988 when we were both trying to get a place on the Olympic team going to Seoul. Anky made it but I did not - she bumped me off at the last trial. But in 1991 we were on the same European Squad together. We won the Team Bronze medal. Anky was 4th individually and I came 7th. I am not from a horsey family but I do come from a sporting family. My father was an international cyclist and went on to coach the Dutch international cycling team.

Horses for me were a coincidence. I was going through a divorce and my friends, as a distraction, asked me to join them hacking on Sundays. I took a few riding lessons so I would not fall off - and I really enjoyed it.

After the divorce I started a riding school. The person who was to run the school let me down so I jumped in to run the business not the horses. However, it was the horses I enjoyed so I decided I would learn as much as I could. I took myself off to a school in Belgium that had horses which excelled in particular movements like piaffe and passage - you could get the feeling of what it would be like. It was very intense training, seven hour days riding and learning theory. At night I would give

My Story

1950 I was born in Holland.

1978 My riding career began with the purchase of a young foal and an 18 month old stallion.

1991 Anky and I rode on the same squad at the European Championships. We won Team Bronze, Individually Anky came 4th and I came 7th.

2000 I was awarded Dressage Trainer of the Year.

2003 The FEI appointed me as a member of the FEI Dressage Commission.

2005 I was appointed Dutch Grand Prix Team Trainer and Chef d'Equipe.

Left *Sjef Janssen, the Dutch Team Trainer, receiving the trophy on behalf of the Dutch team winning the Nations Cup at the CDIO Rotterdam 2009, six points clear of the British Team who placed second*
Opposite, top *Both Sjef and Anky are trainers and often when not riding, Anky is on the sidelines helping her students, many of whom compete against her*
Opposite, right *Anky, Sjef and Salinero's groom, Willeke wait for the final scores to be announced at the 2008 World Cup Final*
Opposite, left *Anky getting advice from her husband/trainer before starting her warm-up at the 2009 CDIO Rotterdam*

private riding lessons. I stayed there for two years.

My training techniques developed over time. My basics are still the classical methods that I was taught initially, you have to show the horse in the classical way according to the FEI book. I was very green when I first started teaching but even then I thought this cannot be the only way to train a horse. I spent a lot of time watching other equestrian events like jumping, the circus and reining, to observe horses. I started to find my own system and noticed that there were other riders and trainers who were also looking for new ways

When Anky and I train together, sometimes the role of trainer/rider gets confused as the lines are not that well defined between us. We are two people who really go for it and work extremely hard, so our working relationship will never be total harmony but we understand this. As a trainer I am open to communication and ideas, not just with Anky but with all of my students and with the horses as well.

I will be in horses forever, I have the bug. Equally I love working and I can't imagine ever not working. We have the children now which was a choice we made. Because children take time you have to give other things up, so Anky decided she would teach less and train less so it means less horses. So that also means I have less training to do. However we have never had so many people from all over the world wanting to train with us. We still have very long days but it is a good mix and I enjoy it. The children are already sitting on their first pony in a Western saddle. I don't want them to ride dressage just yet - they have to learn to have fun and develop a seat first.

Salinero
The Horse

A day in the life

Salinero loves bananas, he is quiet in his stable but he remains alert all the time. He first came to us when he was six years old and was quite nervous. His father, Salieri, who produced many good show jumpers, was also like this. During the first year you could not go into Salinero's stable without him running into the corner. But he is not like that now. It took a year to get his trust and it took many years to get him used to all the travelling and different stabling venues. Salinero would always go well in the competitions but he would be very tense internally, he still is but the older he is getting the less nervous he is. Bonfire was like this as well. Many people thought this tension was a result of our training techniques but it is actually the type of horse we tend to pick. Salinero is very motivated and when he knows the competition is on he wants to get going. This is the sort of horse we like. The good ones are always a little on the edge. It seems to go hand in hand with quality -

Above *Anky and Salinero after another fine performance at Windsor*
Right *Anky and Salinero executing flying changes*
Opposite, Left *Anky and Salinero draped in the Champion's rug at the CDIO Rotterdam*
Opposite, Right *Anky and Salinero winners of the Grand Prix Kur at 2008 CDIO Rotterdam. With success comes the press and photographers are always keen to take pictures of this attractive duo*

Salinero's Competition Highlights

2003 1st Grand Prix Kur at CDI-W Mechelen, 1st Grand Prix Kur at CDI-W Maastricht.

2004 1st World Cup Final Dusseldorf, Individual Gold medal Athens Olympics, 1st Grand Prix Kur at CDIO 's Hertogenbosch.

2005 1st World Cup Final Las Vegas, 1st Nations Cup at CDIO Aachen, 1st Grand Prix and Kur CDI-W London Olympia, 1st Grand Prix Special and Kur European Championships at Hagen, 1st Grand Prix and Kur at CDI-W Mechelen, 1st Grand Prix and Kur at CDI-W Maastricht, 1st Grand Prix and Special at CDI Gelderland, 1st Grand Prix and Kur at CDI-W Dusseldorf, 1st Grand Prix and Kur at CDI-W 's Hertogenbosch, Dutch National Champion

2006 1st World Cup Final Amsterdam, 1st World Equestrian Games Aachen, 1st Grand Prix (world record) at CHIO Rotterdam, 1st Grand Prix Kur (world record) and Grand Prix at CDI-W 's Hertogenbosch.

2007 Individual and Team Gold European Championships at Turin, Italy Dutch National Champion.

2008 1st World Cup Final Brabant Holland, Team Silver, Individual Gold medal at the Beijing Olympics.

2009 1st Grand Prix 3rd Kur CDI-W 's Hertogenbosch, Team Silver, Bronze medal Kur at European Dressage Championships at Windsor.

Bonfire and Salinero's personalities are quite different in comparison to other horses.

Salinero goes out of his stable five times each day and as close to nature as possible. He is ridden, hand-walked twice, hand-grazed and groomed. He used to get turned out with a pony but he got injured so now he is hand-grazed instead. We are not keen to have too many horses as we like to spend lots of time with each one looking after them and this takes a lot of staff at this level. Sometimes Sjef and I do chip in and do our share of the hand-walking. At shows Salinero is hacked on a long rein in the morning, or at least several hours before his class, to give him confidence. Before he goes into the competition he is ridden intensely and then goes into the arena. The timing of his routine at shows is very precise to prevent him from getting over excited.

When we initially spotted Salinero's talent we thought he would be a good match for one of our students American, Tess Guilder. We had no idea the greatest part of his potential was still untapped and after working with him for a while we eventually purchased him for ourselves. Salinero has come such a long way in such a short time achieving surprising wins that we did not think he would be ready for, such as winning the Olympic Gold when he was only 10 years old- not bad for a horse that was bred to jump.

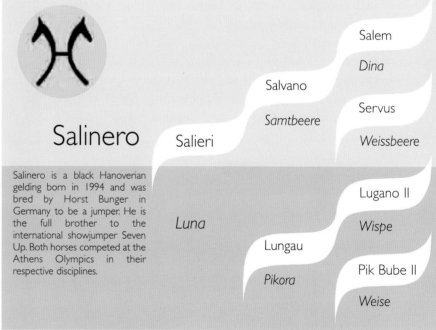

Salinero

Salinero is a black Hanoverian gelding born in 1994 and was bred by Horst Bunger in Germany to be a jumper. He is the full brother to the international showjumper Seven Up. Both horses competed at the Athens Olympics in their respective disciplines.

Salieri — Salvano — Salem / Dina
Salieri — Samtbeere — Servus / Weissbeere
Luna — Lungau — Lugano II / Wispe
Luna — Pikora — Pik Bube II / Weise

Anky's Kur

Having placed first in so many Kurs Anky has been labelled 'Queen of the Kur' by the international media. In 2006 Salinero established a new World Record of 87.925% for this event and then later that year they set a new World Record in the Grand Prix of 81.33%. Anky's early Kur music was composed by Dutch duo Victor Kerkhof and Cees Slings. They relied heavily on movie themes and popular music for inspiration to create Kurs which helped Anky to win many coveted 'dressage to music' awards. Every step of Anky's Kur routine is choreographed with the rhythm and beat of the music matching exactly the footfall of her horse's paces. Countless numbers of hours are spent preparing the Kur so that it is perfect when performed in front of the judges and audience. With Anky's success Kerkhof and Slings found themselves much in demand from other riders to prepare music for them too. Anky has since had music composed for her and Salinero by the Dutch born, internationally recognised concert pianist Wibi Soerjadi. This creative partnership has again proved to be very successful, with Anky and Salinero winning the Individual Gold medal at the Beijing Olympics to Soerjadi's *Dance of Devotion*. So popular is Anky's music that there is great demand to buy her Kur music on CD.

Dressage and Showjumping in Rotterdam

The Rotterdam CHIO is the largest and considered by many to be the best international outdoor show in the Netherlands. For many years Rotterdam has hosted the only CHIO level competition in Holland. Founded in 1948 on the grounds of the riding school 'de Rotterdamsche Manege'. Initially it was military personnel and members of wealthy families which took home the honours but today participants come from all over Europe and from many different backgrounds to compete in dressage and show jumping. To date Anky van Grunsven on several of her equine partners has won more awards at CHIO Rotterdam than any other competitor.

Piaffe

Lisa Wilcox and Relevant

The piaffe is a highly collected, cadenced, elevated movement giving the impression of the horse remaining 'in place' for twelve to fifteen steps. The horse's back is supple and elastic. The quarters are slightly lowered, the haunches with active hocks are well-engaged, giving great freedom, lightness and mobility to the shoulders and forehand. Each diagonal pair of feet is raised and returned to the ground alternately, with an even cadence.

Here we see the utterly charming Relevant with his elegant and beautiful American rider, Lisa Wilcox. The feeling we derive from this picture is that the horse appears to be performing this most difficult of all the dressage movements almost completely of his own accord and is merely being 'guided' by his sympathetic rider. There is the look of total ease and fluidity in this picture with a complete absence of any force or pressure being exerted by either horse or rider.

The magic of this illustration is the great height and expression of the steps achieved by Relevant as a result of the enormous impulsion he can generate from his hind legs, coupled with the very light control exerted by Lisa. Relevant is able to demonstrate the highest quality piaffe, with assured ease and grace.

Relevant seems to trot almost on the spot but with a desire to move forwards, expressed so clearly in this picture, whilst fulfiling virtually all of the technical criteria, such as the clarity of the diagonal legs, the hoof of the raised front leg reaching halfway up the cannon bone of the supporting front leg, and the hoof of the raised hind leg reaching the height of the fetlock of the supporting hind leg. The straightness of his body position and the correct carriage of his head and neck all with the confident acceptance of the bridle. The carrying power of the well-flexed hocks and engaged hind legs that are working through a soft and swinging back with a relaxed tail, demonstrate suppleness and elasticity with the apparent absence of either physical or mental tension. This graceful impression of horse and rider dancing on the spot is complemented even further by the obvious lightness of the rider's aids and the truly forwards contact that is being offered by the reins, resulting in a picture of true excellence. Lisa's position is so light, she is sitting so softly in the saddle and her legs are simply next to his side. The well-educated Relevant knows what to do and enjoys doing it.

On the many occasions I have judged this combination I have noticed that Relevant, despite his immense talent and possession of the classic look of an assured stallion, draws so much of his confidence from his rider. Lisa is an extremely gifted and confident rider who transmits her secure feelings onto her partner and together they have produced some outstanding tests.

There are not many breeding stallions who firstly compete at this level of international dressage and who can fulfil their breeding obligations and then come out and produce high quality movements like this. It is a testament of the co-operation, organization and commitment between Relevant's owner, rider and trainer in their goal to see him achieve success in the dressage arena. It is difficult enough to plan an international Grand Prix schedule with a mare or gelding but, with the added dimension of a breeding schedule thrown in it can become a nail-biting experience. The consistently good results Relevant has been able to sustain have made the efforts worthwhile and will contribute to a secure breeding schedule.

Lisa Wilcox

The Rider

My most memorable test

The Grand Prix Special at Stuttgart in 2002 will always be the most memorable ride for me. It was where Relevant and I beat the world's best competitors on German soil. So unexpected was our win that there was an uncomfortable delay before the prize giving because the organizers could not find a copy of the American anthem. As is customary for all winners of this prestigious event, Relevant and I have our names eternally displayed on the 'Stuttgart Wall', the only American to ever do so. It is difficult to pinpoint what triggered such an amazing performance from Reli that day, he is normally tense at indoor competitions which is why we never took part in the World Cup Qualifiers, which are all held indoors. Riding in front of the educated Stuttgart audience, who are quick to express their appreciation with great emotional applause and whistling when they see a good performance, would normally unsettle my boy. The warm-up went very well, something I would superstitiously never confess to before entering the arena. During the test Relevant felt great, his piaffe felt so solid and balanced. I counted the required 15 steps and never worried that his rhythm would change as I might have done in other tests. The test flowed and was flawless. We waited until all the results were posted - I had tears in my eyes. I was so proud of my boy - to hear the American anthem in Germany meant so much to me.

My daily routine

When I started working for Gestüt Vorwerk, the Olympic Gold medallist Nicole Uphoff and I trained the

Above *Lisa Wilcox on the stallion Relevant. Happy with her test at Aachen 2003*
Opposite, left *Lisa modelling for Pikeur*
Opposite, right *'One of my favourite moments -'on the podium at the Hickstead European Championships 2003' with some of the world's best riders.' l. to r: Beatriz Ferrer-Salat riding Beauvalais won Team Silver and Individual Bronze in the Grand Prix, Ulla Salzgeber riding Rusty won Team Gold and Individual Gold, Jan Brink riding Bjorsells Briar won Silver in the Grand Prix Kur and Individual Bronze and Lisa Wilcox riding Relevant won Individual Silver, Silver in the Grand Prix Special and Bronze in the Grand Prix Kur*

My Story

1966 Born in Colorado on 8th Sept. I learned to ride Western first.

1980s Studied equine science and marketing at university. I was introduced to dressage by my then husband, Jan Ebeling.

1994 I moved to Europe and for 12 years worked in some of the best stables, rode some of the best stallions and was taught by the best trainers.

2000 Achieved the German instructor's Bereiter.

2004 I left Vorwerk for Dr. Schatzmann's stable in Switzerland.

2006 I returned to the US to live and continue riding and competing.

My secret to success - I make an effort to ensure my horses enjoy and understand their work, look forward to being ridden and want to co-operate. And if the 'Do it with a Smile' is part of it - then it's dressage.'

stallions together. When Nicole left, I became the No. 1 rider and at one point I was riding 12 horses a day. This meant an 8am start and not finishing until 4 or 5pm. In the evening I would have just enough energy for dinner then straight to bed, feeling rather burnt out. Mrs Vorwerk-Happ approached Ernst Hoyos to be our trainer. The knowledge and confidence Ernst gave me was unparalleled to anything in my life. Together we rode and trained all the horses and in this new arrangement I was able to ride more of the up-and-coming youngsters. I had the time and energy to give them my deepest thoughts and to do other things besides riding such as modelling for Pikeur, which is great fun and which I still do twice a year. Having time to myself is important.

How my riding career began

My parents ran a cattle ranch in Colorado so it isn't surprising that I learned to ride Western first. My six brothers and sisters actually did round up the cattle just like the cowboys. My interest in dressage began when I met my first husband, Jan Ebeling. He had a wonderful horse, Funny Boy, that I learned the advanced movements on. It wasn't long before I was hooked on dressage and in 1993, aged 27, I trained with Herbert Rehbein for four months. I went home briefly and then

My Competition Highlights

2000 1st Bundeschampion for 6 year olds, 2nd Grand Prix, Bremen on Rohdiamant.

2001 4th round 1 Nurnberg Burg Pokal, 1st Prix St Georges and Intermediaire I, 1st Prix St Georges at CDI Lingen on Royal Diamond, 3rd Grand Prix, 4th Kur at CDI Dusseldorf, 4th Grand Prix, 3rd Kur at CDI Lingen, 5th Grand Prix, 4th Special at CDI Bremen on Rohdiamant, 1st Prix St Georges at CDI Bremen, 4th Prix St Georges, 2nd Intermediaire I at CDI Lingen on Regal Dancer.

2002 4th Nurnberg Burg Pokal Finals, 1st Prix St Georges, 1st Intermediaire I at CDI Oldenburg, 2nd Prix St Georges, 1st Intermediaire I at CDN Bremen, 2nd Prix St Georges, 3rd Intermediaire at CHIO Aachen on Royal Diamond.

2003 5th Prix St Georges at CDN Meppen, 7th Class S at CDI Norten-Hardenberg on Danny Wilde.

2004 7th Prix St Georges, 5th Intermediaire I on Danny Wilde, 3rd Prix St Georges and Intermediaire I on Jazz Time at CDI Olfen, 1st Prix St Georges on Jazz Time at CDN Meppen, 1st Prix St Georges and Intermediaire I on Jazz Time at CDN Bad Salzuflen.

returned to Europe where I remained for the next 12 years. The first few years I moved from stable to stable learning as much as I could from many of the top trainers and then 'the tap on the shoulder' it was Mrs. Gudula Vorwerk-Happ sitting behind me at the 1997 European Championships in Verden. She offered me a dream job - to be one of her riders at the oldest and most prestigious stud in Germany, Gestüt Vorwerk in Oldenburg. Everything I became in the competitive world was due to the excellent training I received from Ernst Hoyos and the fabulous stallions I was privileged to ride. After 7 years winning international competitions for Vorwerk, I accepted an offer to train young horses for Dr. Schatzmann's stable in Switzerland. It was difficult to leave 'my boys' at Vorwerk but I felt it was the right decision to move on. The focus at Dr. Schatzmann's was to train young horses to sell, which I found difficult as I was so used to long relationships with the breeding stallions. Eventually the yearning for my family, warmer winters and friends strengthened and I moved home to the United States in February 2006.

I love being back, I am so busy giving clinics, running my own farm, training promising young horses and riders and basically putting all I have learned to good use.

Ernst Hoyos

The Trainer

My Story

1955 Born in Austria, Ernst's interest in riding began on Icelandic horses that his family still breed today along with Thoroughbreds for eventing.

1972 At 17 Ernst joined the Spanish Riding School of Vienna where he remained for 29 years.

2002 Ernst left the Riding School and Vienna and moved to Germany, establishing himself as one of the best dressage trainers of his day. Some of his star pupils have included world class riders such as Ulla Salzgeber and Lisa Wilcox.

Ernst Hoyos is famous for his in-hand work and his understanding of young horses. His training methods are steeped in 430 years of tradition at the Spanish Riding School complimented with his own ideas which he feels advance the classical principles of riding.

Training Lisa and Relevant

I have a very defined system of riding that I have developed as part of my 29 years with the Spanish Riding School, coupled with my own experiences and understanding, which varies for each horse depending on their age and abilities. I put a lot of emphasis on the rider's seat and the rider's ability to balance the horse, so much so that if I am riding Relevant I try to mimic Lisa's body weight so as not to alter the lightness and sensitivity she has already established with him. If I use a heavier weight or a full seat when riding Relevant then he will learn instead to respond to the heavier weight. The ultimate goal is the aids should be unnoticeable to anyone watching. As Relevant gets older he is more balanced and it takes less weight to get him to react - this is what we strive for.

Lisa rides in the classical way, her weight stays in the centre of the saddle, never sacrificing her position, and she always rides like she is in a competition, always striving for perfection - how to make the movements better than last time. When we are establishing the bend, Lisa sits deep in the saddle and steps into the inside stirrup, putting more weight on the inside seat bone - she does not shift her balance but sits straight. Relevant will move away from this weight creating a bend through his rib cage so pressing the calf against the side is not necessary.

We use our voice in training, clucking or talking which supports using less seat. Strong stomach muscles are essential for strong back muscles, so think sitting in a slightly forward position with shoulders back but not hollowed. This is how Lisa keeps Relevant in front of the leg - which is loose and not driving all the time. The leg must be used sparingly but quickly so when you do want a reaction you get one, as the horse has not become bored with its use. Horses will naturally want to slow down when you continually squeeze with your leg because they become tight through the rib cage.

Lisa's body control is important. A rider has to sit up straight but not be rigid through the shoulders. Breathing through the lower stomach helps the upper body to relax. In this way Lisa can find that sensitive balance between the ever changing flow of energy that travels from the horse's mouth over the back to the hind leg and back again and the amount of pressure Relevant can tolerate. If you have dead hands and a stiff upper body, the horse will not move forward or it will move forward onto the forehand. The rider's upper body must be relaxed so the horse can move away from the weight and into the contact of soft hands. Relevant has his moments, as all horses do, when he would prefer to run away from a piaffe or a passage. Establishing this balance between position and pressure and making the rider's position light makes it easier for Relevant to do the movement over his back and to establish the message.

Relevant is trained in the same way by Lisa everyday, five to six times each week, he may go for a hack on one of these days. When it is breeding season then he is not ridden so much. The priority of Vorwerk is breeding first and then competitions.

Relevant ideally executes piaffe with good contact and with Lisa sitting balanced in the centre of the saddle. However, there are times in training and in competitions when the horse's mental and physical state require the rider to allow the horse to almost do the movement with no pressure at all. It is a testament to Lisa's training and riding ability to produce such good Piaffe with virtually no contact. The happiness and willingness of her horses to work for her is important to Lisa.

Lisa's tips for successful riding: Always give as much time as is required in your daily riding to let the horse respond. Don't restrict yourself by time, have a plan not a timetable. Never ride a tired horse, they will be too distressed to teach anything to. Be consistent in day to day training, do the same routine every day so they know what to expect. If things aren't going right, check your body position.

Opposite *Ernst Hoyos, once a member of the Spanish Riding School of Vienna and now trainer to international dressage riders such as Lisa Wilcox and Ulla Salzgeber*
Above *Ernst Hoyos and Lisa Wilcox giving a clinic at United States Dressage Federation symposium held in Dallas in 2003*
Left *Ernst Hoyos and Rudolph Zeilinger coaching their students from ring-side before the Grand Prix at CHIO Aachen 2009*

Relevant
The Horse

A day in the life

Relevant is one of the most successful dressage stallions in the world. He was a major contributor to the Americans historic Silver Team medal win at the World Championships in Jerez in 2002. He is such a relaxed horse but always gives his best, even when training at home. Standing 16.3 hands high, a bright chestnut, he is my 'Cary Grant' on four hooves, he is so unbelievably charming and accommodating. His most attractive aspect is that he has no idea how beautiful and talented he is. There is absolutely no ego about him and he relied on me for encouragement to do his best. Since I have returned to the United States, Relevant is being shown successfully by Dutch rider, Marlies van Baalen.

During the breeding season Relevant's competition and training schedule had to be worked out carefully as collection had to happen each morning before he was ridden or competed as exercise can reduce a stallion's sperm count. Breeding did not interfere with his riding but the distance of the competition from the stallion station was a major factor when deciding what competitions to attend. Sometimes if it was a major show we would travel to a nearby collection yard and then return him to the competition. The timing of this was often a nail-biting experience.

The indoor arena is the venue where, for years, Relevant had been presented to potential breeders and so naturally he would get worked up at the prospect. This is why he missed out on the World Cup Qualifiers and the Finals, which were always held indoors. However, it is also this excitement which makes Relevant such an expressive Grand Prix champion.

Any breeding facility will tell you that breeding comes first but not many facilities would have a breeding stallion that also competes and wins at International Grand Prix. If they did have such a stallion, they would rely on frozen semen. But since Gestüt Vorwerk had their own collection facility and they wanted to sell live semen, this was the path we decided to follow.

True to his nature, Relevant was a gentle boy in his

stable. He would be hand grazed every day on the lush grass around the farm. After a while he would get nervous but would settle down again to graze. At Gestüt Vorwerk there were always mares and foals coming and going so he was easily distracted. Never was Relevant in an environment where he could just let go and totally relax. Either he was concentrating on his dressage or being prepared to cover mares.

When time permitted I would groom Reli myself. I could always tell what sort of mood he was in because if he was in a bad mood he would play with his mouth when on the cross-ties. I spoiled Relevant with carrots, apples and special molasses horse cookies, but his favourite was sugar cubes. When he was in a bad mood he would never take a sugar from me but he would always accept a sugar from Ernst, regardless of his mood. Ernst enjoyed proving this point to me. Relevant loved his big muscly neck, along with his withers and shoulders brushed, but not his ticklish stomach.

The care provided by the grooms at Gestüt Vorwerk

Relevant's Competition Highlights

1998 Winner of Nurnberg Burg Pokal, Winner of Small Tour CHIO Aachen.

2001 Best Stallion in Zwolle NED, six further 1st Grand Prix and Special at: Oldenburg, 2nd Grand Prix and Kur at CDI Frankfurt, Wiesbaden, 1st Grand Prix and Kur at CDI Bremen, Oldenburg, Bad Salzuflen (free style) and Balve.

2002 5th Individual and Team Silver at WEG in Jerez, 4th Nations Cup, 4th Kur in Aachen, 5th Kur at World Cup in Frankfurt, 1st Grand Prix and Kur at CDI Lingen, 1st Grand Prix and Kur at CDI Frankfurt, 2nd Grand Prix, 1st Special at Stuttgart, 1st Grand Prix and Special at CDI Oldenburg, 5th Grand Prix at CDN Bremen.

2003 Silver Individual medal at European Championships at Hickstead, 6th Grand Prix Special at CDN Bad Salzuflen, 1st Grand Prix and Special CDN Meppen, 2nd Grand Prix, 6th Special at CDI Norten-Hardenberg, 2nd Grand Prix, Special and Kur, Gold Nations Cup at CDIO Aachen.

2004 Bronze Team, 18th Grand Prix at Athens Olympics. 1st Grand Prix at Oldenburg, 1st Grand Prix,, 6th Special at CDI Lingen, 1st Grand Prix and Special at CDI Oldenburg, 1st Grand Prix at CDN Hanover.

Relevant

Relevant was born in 1991, his breeder was Heinz Luers from Westerstede, GER. He is a licensed Oldenburg stallion but he is approved for Westphalian, Hanovarian and Rheinlander societies as well. Relevant was bought privately by Gudula Vorwerk-Happ as a four yr old and was standing at the Gestüt Vorwerk in Cappeln GER.

Rubinstein — Rosenkavalier — Romadour II / Diva*; Antine — Angelo xx / Dodona

Havanna — Goldlowe — Gotthard / La Paris; Hallett II — Venator xx / Hallett

was second to none. Relevant's needs were always tended to with no expense or time spared. I believe that he was and still is very happy in his work, his breeding responsibilities and in his life. I miss my 'Cary Grant' but I know he will be treated like the king that he is forever.

Opposite *Relevant and Lisa completing their Kur at the European Championships at Hickstead where they won the Silver Medal behind Ulla Salzgeber and Rusty. Relevant is known not only for his amazing paces but also his well developed neck*
Left *Relevant and Lisa executing a beautiful ground covering trot half-pass at the 2003 European Championships*

Lisa Wilcox and Relevant

Taking a quiet moment away from the pressures of the competition arena and training, Lisa and Relevant find time to relax and enjoy their beautiful surroundings at Gestüt Vorwerk in Cappeln, Germany. In 2004, Lisa left Germany for stables in Switzerland before returning home to the United States in 2006. Relevant was moved to Stables Dressage Van Baalen where he was ridden successfully by Marlies Van Baalen. In 2009 Gestüt Vorwerk was sold to Austrian Olympic dressage rider, Sissy Max-Theurer. The new occupants intend to preserve Vorwerk's long standing traditional charm.

Since Lisa's return to the United States she has been in great demand both as a rider and trainer. Her experiences gained from twelve years spent among Europe's best horsemen has put her in a position where several top performance farms in the United States want to put her skills and knowledge to good use. Lisa has been competing extensively in Florida and hopes to join the International Dressage scene once again.

Passage

Andreas Helgstrand and Blue Hors Matine

This is a measured, very collected, elevated and cadenced trot. It is characterized by a pronounced engagement of the hindquarters, a more accentuated flexion of the knees and hocks, and the graceful elasticity of the movement. Each diagonal pair of legs is raised and returned to the ground alternately, with cadence and a prolonged suspension. In principle, the height of the toe of the raised forefoot should be level with the middle of the cannon bone of the other supporting foreleg. The toe of the raised hind leg should be slightly above the fetlock joint of the other supporting hind leg. The neck should be raised and gracefully arched with poll as the highest point and the nose line close to the vertical. The horse should remain light and soft 'on the bit' in true 'self-carriage' and perfect balance with the impulsion remaining lively and pronounced.

One of the most exciting combinations to hit the Dressage scene in recent years is Andreas Helgstrand and the outstandingly expressive grey mare, Blue Hors Matine. In this shot of the duo performing the Passage it is extraordinary to see the energy and height of these steps. The way Matine springs effortlessly through the air with her enormous impulsion and huge amount of suspension whilst remaining completely balanced and 'featherlight' in both her carriage and footfalls certainly makes an impressive picture.

One of the reasons that this pair seem to have reached the hearts of the spectators and judges alike, is that all this energy and expression seems to be completely 'on offer' from this wonderfully athletic mare, without the slightest effort being made by her talented rider, whose elegant position brings the finishing touch to this dazzling picture.

When heading the leader board in the Grand Prix section of the World Equestrian Games in Aachen 2006, they created a real 'buzz' in the spectators stands with their electric and athletic performance, becoming one of the crowd's all time favourites and certainly the talk of the show. When they performed their Kur later the crowd were treated to another spectacular display. The bounce, spring and athleticism seen in her paces in the earlier Grand Prix appeared even more expressive when set against her explosive pop music.

Andreas, keeping his aids very subtle, appeared to be perfectly at ease in the saddle. Matine was on fire and went from one transition to the next completely in time with the music. When dressage is this creative and the horse's movements executed with so much expression you don't have to be an expert judge to appreciate what good dressage is all about. With only the smallest of mistakes in the execution of a couple of her exercises, Matine came an honourable second just behind Anky van Grunsven and Salinero. In her short dressage career, Matine made an everlasting impression on everyone who watched her perform. It is a pity that injury has since kept this very talented mare away from the competition arena, as there was certainly much more to come from this young and exciting combination.

Rudolph Zeilinger

The Trainer

Training Andreas and Matine

I have been training Andreas since 2002. I was already the trainer of Lars Petersen who was the head rider at Blue Hors before he moved to the United States. When Andreas was employed to take Petersen's place, I continued as his trainer. The German system of training is quite similar to the Danish system so Andreas and I get on very well. We have a good relationship and can talk openly about things.

Andreas accomplished more than anyone expected in his first years at Blue Hors and then in 2004, he had such a successful competition year, but a very hectic one, campaigning two Grand Prix horses. At Norton-Hardenberg, his first time out with these horses at Grand Prix level, he qualified both of them for the Danish Olympic team. Andreas is a very focused rider and very talented. At the big competitions he totally immerses himself in his work for the eight minutes or so while riding the test. We work together mainly on the technical side of riding the Grand Prix. Andreas is very motivated and tries to make every competition better than the one before. He is very cool and rarely gets nervous before a test.

When Matine was young, she did not have the big paces she later became famous for. She always found the piaffe and passage easy but it was a surprise to everyone how extravagant her paces became. As the piaffe and passage became more balanced and expressive, her other paces like the canter, half-passes, walk and trot also improved. There was some controversy over the swishing of her tail. On her part it was never a sign of evasion or tension - some mares are just like that when you touch

Above *Rudolph Zeilinger trainer of the Danish International Team and coach of many other successful professional and amateur riders*
Opposite, top *Andreas and Rudolph discussing competition schedules. When Andreas is riding several horses at one competition and Rudolph is training many students at the same competition, timing is so important to ensure success*
Opposite, bottom *Matine was famous for her athletic piaffe and passage but she was also exemplary in her other paces, such as the extended trot, which she is demonstrating here at the World Equestrian Games at Aachen*

My Story

1963 I was born in Ansbach in Bavaria, Germany.

1978 I began my training with Willie Schultheiss which lasted for ten years. It was his insight into riding that formed the basis of my own philosophy to teaching and training.

1990s I established my own yard, Zeilinger-Sporthorses Ltd located in Emsburen, Weser-Ems where I train both professional and amateur riders along with horses of all ages and talents.

1999 I became coach of the Danish International Dressage squad and over the years the team and individual riders enjoyed many successes including the Team Bronze medal at the Beijing Olympics.

2006 My riding career was replaced by my busy teaching and training schedules which I still thoroughly enjoy.

Rudolph's Competition Highlights

2000 1st Grand Prix Kur CDI-W Amsterdam, 1st Grand Prix Kur CDI-W Mechelen on Livijno.

2001 2nd Grand Prix and Kur at CDI Lingen, 2nd World Cup Finals at Vilhelmsborg, 6th Grand Prix, 5th Special, 3rd Kur at German Dressage Championships on Livijno.

2004 8th Grand Prix, 10th Kur at CDI Bremen Euroclassics on Festival, 2nd Short Grand Prix at CDI Munster, Rolinck Cup on World of Dreams.

2005 1st Grand Prix at CDI Lingen, 5th Grand Prix, 7th Special at CDN Munster on Festival.

2006 3rd Grand Prix, 9th Kur at CDI Wiesbaden, 6th Grand Prix, 4th Kur at CDN Hamburg on Francis.

them with your leg. I, personally, have ridden Matine many times and there is no tension in her. Under saddle Matine is very normal but handling her on the ground, she is full of energy. Luckily she does not suffer from the moodiness that some mares are prone to. She is always ready to work and enjoys it.

I also coach the Danish National squad, of which Andreas has been a member for some time. We have clinics every two weeks. Many of the Danish team members live in Germany or Holland so it is not difficult to get to them. Before my role as trainer took over, I used to compete quite a lot and I have participated in two World Cup Finals, The Olympics and European Championships. Now there is no time to compete as I spend most of my time training others, which I thoroughly enjoy. When my riders do well, I get the same enjoyment and satisfaction as if I was riding. I run my own stables at Emsburen, Weser-Ems and have very good stable managers, which allows me to travel to other centres to give lessons.

Matine

The Horse

A day in the life

Matine was not born at the Blue Hors Stud but was purchased directly from her breeder as a four year old, so she was already at Blue Hors when I began working there. One of my first tasks was to prepare Matine for the five year old classes, which she won, and then the six year old classes, which she also won. When Matine turned seven, she became very difficult. At that age all horses experience more pressure in their training because this is a time when they have to learn so much. I think because Matine was so sensitive and so talented, when the pressure was put on her, she responded badly. So at seven she was put on the Blue Hors sales list because of this attitude. Matine was very hot, but in comparison to all horses at the age of seven or eight, she was not too bad. Sometimes I felt like I was the only person who sensed she had a lot more to give, especially in her collected work. I discussed this with my trainer and he said maybe one day if you are lucky you can go around and get 70% for the Grand Prix but not more. So I said 'I will show them'.

Matine was always hand walked and walked under saddle to calm her and to warm her up for her training session gradually. When she was in training she was not turned out because she had too much energy and we thought she might hurt herself - by kicking, bucking and running so fast in her paddock.

It was fun bringing Matine on and in the end, as she grew older, she did change a lot. I tried to get into her mindset and if I was successful, then she would do anything for me. A few years later, after continuous hard work, when Matine was only nine she put on a spectacular performance at the World Equestrian Games, held at Aachen, by coming first in the Grand Prix and second in the Kur. It was this Kur which millions of her fans and supporters have watched in astonishment, again and again, on the internet, of Matine bouncing through her piaffe and passage

Above *Blue Hors Matine looking fresh and alert after just completing her Grand Prix Kur*
Opposite, top *Umbrellas up - both the World Equestrian Games and the Olympics are held outdoors so horses and riders must be used to competing in all kinds of weather*
Opposite, bottom *So concentrated was Matine on Andreas that she did not seem to notice the audience and the swarm of photographers until the final salute*

Matine's Competition Highlights

2003 Danish Champion 6 yr old.

2005 1st Grand Prix at CDI Wiesbaden, 2nd Grand Prix at CDI Lingen, 4th Intermediaire II CHIO Aachen, 1st Grand Prix and Special at CDI-W Vilhelmsborg, 1st Grand Prix and Special at Dalumgard Rideklub.

2006 Danish Dressage Champion, 1st Grand Prix, Team Bronze medal Special, Silver medal Kur, Bronze medal Grand Prix Special at World Equestrian Games, Aachen, 7th Grand Prix, 1st Special at CHIO Aachen, 1st Grand Prix, 2nd Special at CDI Wiesbaden, 1st Grand Prix, 5th Kur at CDI-W Stockholm.

2007 2nd Grand Prix and Kur at CDI-W 's Hertogenbosch.

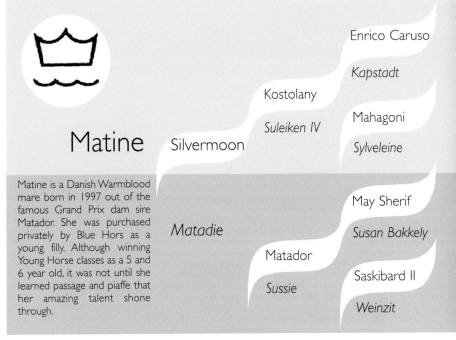

Matine

			Enrico Caruso
		Kostolany	Kapstadt
	Silvermoon	Suleiken IV	Mahagoni
			Sylveleine
Matadie			May Sherif
		Matador	Susan Bakkely
	Sussie		Saskibard II
			Weinzit

Matine is a Danish Warmblood mare born in 1997 out of the famous Grand Prix dam sire Matador. She was purchased privately by Blue Hors as a young filly. Although winning Young Horse classes as a 5 and 6 year old, it was not until she learned passage and piaffe that her amazing talent shone through.

movements. Matine then qualified for the 2007 World Cup Finals to be held in Las Vegas. Her flight over was fine but I received a telephone call from the groom telling me that Matine had fallen off the lorry ramp and that her leg was swelling up. I went down to see her and her leg was a little stiff but not that much. When I returned her to her stable, the leg started to enlarge. At the vet check, the following day, the leg had swollen much more and I knew then there was something wrong, so we withdrew from the competition.

It has been several years now since Matine was injured and Blue Hors were trying to build her up again gradually, but her injury just would not heal completely. Matine is now enjoying her life living with a herd of other mares and will soon become a broodmare.

Blue Hors Matine and Andreas Helgstrand

The most watched Equestrian video on You Tube is of this magnificent duo competing in the Grand Prix Kur at the World Equestrian Games at Aachen in 2006. Matine dazzled the judges, the audience and the world with her amazing energetic piaffe and passage movements coupled with the sounds of *Lady Marmalade*. Commentators covering the event claimed the atmosphere in the arena changed from subdued to a charged-up rock concert. The audience with over 50,000 spectators clapped in time to the rhythm of Matine's music. Unfortunately, since Matine's accident at the World Cup Finals in 2008, the dressage world has been patiently waiting for her return. There have been plans for a comeback which have not materialized as her owners feel her fitness and well being are paramount and so Matine has now been retired from competitions and will resume her life as a broodmare. Andreas has since left Blue Hors to establish his own equestrian establishment.

Helgstrand Dressage

The Helgstrand family moved into their new premises Moegelmosegaard in the summer of 2009. It is the realisation of a dream for Andreas as he will have his family, the stallions, teaching and training facilities all in one location. Moegelmosegaard will develop into one of the finest equestrian centres in Denmark offering not only quality young horses for sale but also established Grand Prix horses. Located in Hammer Bakker, an area of outstanding natural beauty in North Jutland, it is conveniently located near the airport of Aalborg.

Piaffe Passage Transition

Ashley Holzer and Pop Art

The transition should be performed where prescribed. Both from the passage into the piaffe and from the piaffe into the passage, the transitions should be fluent and clearly defined, without the slightest hesitation or resistance. The cadence/rhythm should be maintained throughout. The horse should remain light and soft 'on the bit' in true self carriage, with the impulsion remaining lively and pronounced. Thereby demonstrating the willingness of the horse to go fluently and effortlessly from one movement to the other without any loss of cadence/rhythm, balance, straightness or energy.

Here we see one of Canada's greatest ambassadors for the sport of dressage, Ashley Holzer, with her charming equestrian partner, Pop Art, showing the piaffe/passage transition. Even from these still illustrations it is easy to see such wonderful energy and expression with complete balance and harmony between the horse and rider. The trusting expression on 'Poppy's' face and the elastic and soft contact that Ashley maintains with the reins is a joy to behold!

In the first shot we see the passage classically demonstrated and in the second shot, having arrived into the piaffe, it is so clear to see the horse's body weight being transferred more on to his hindquarters with the hind legs stepping further under the centre of gravity, with the obvious lowering of the croup and the increased bending of the joints of the hind legs.

What is impossible to see from the still photographs is the 'clockwork' rhythm that this pair manage to maintain through these transitions, both from the passage to the piaffe and from the piaffe to the passage. These transitions carry the potential for a full ten marks and it has been my pleasure, as a judge, to award this ultimate score to Ashley and Pop Art on more than one occasion.

This harmonious combination continue to inspire up and coming dressage riders, particularly the young throughout the World, but especially in North America, with their sportsmanlike attitude and sense of fair play. There are several highly talented and motivated riders in Canada, who, I'm sure, take heart from the great success that Ashley brings back to the country.

Canada has produced other great dressage riders in the past such as Christilot Boylen, and Cindy O'Neil to mention but a few. As better and better riders and trainers emerge in Canada their experiences and knowledge have been utilized to encourage other up and coming dressage riders from Pony Riders through to Young Riders. Already a base of young talent can be seen emerging, creating a solid foundation from which riders can be chosen to represent their country.

In the early days, Ashley spent much time training in Europe, with horses funded by herself and her very benevolent sponsors. To train with the best is one thing, to compete against the best, is quite another matter, especially when the best competitors and competitions are held in Europe. The expense of flying your horse to these venues often limits the frequency with which some North American competitors can attend. However, whenever Ashley is up against the best in the world, she and Pop Art, more often than not, find themselves right up there with the leaders.

Ashley Holzer

The Rider

Above *Ashley Holzer*
Opposite, left *Ashley and Pop Art in the warm up arena. Ashley is one of very few Grand Prix riders who wears a hard hat during their warm up at competitions*
Opposite, right *Ashley getting the thumbs up from her husband, Rusty, during her Grand Prix test at the CDIO at Hickstead 2009*

My Story

1963 I was born 10th October in Toronto Ontario, Canada.

1970's When I turned 13 I was given my first horse Gloria, we did eventing and dressage.

1979 A few years later I had my first taste of international competitions riding a leased horse.

1981 Johann Hinnemann and Willi Schultheiss agreed to train me in Germany, when I returned Evi Pracht became my trainer at her yard in Cedar Valley Ontario, Canada.

1984 I was selected as the reserve rider for the Canadian Olympic team that went to Los Angeles.

1988 At the Seoul Olympics I won the Team Bronze medal on Reipo.

1994 My soon to be husband, Rusty, and I moved to Riverdale Equestrian Centre in New York City.

I've always thought Pop Art, or Poppy as we call him, was special although my husband kept questioning if he really was so special. Poppy was great at Prix St. Georges and remained unbeaten at that level but I didn't realise how special he really was until the first year we were doing Grand Prix. Poppy finds all of the Grand Prix movements so easy. And he is not a tricky horse with attitude, just a lovely animal which makes riding him a joy. I couldn't pick one particular test to date that was our favourite, although I've thought the freestyles we have done recently in 2009 have been our best, particularly the Kurs at the CDI's in Florida. This improved consistency in our performances I feel is due to the fact that we have been out competing quite a lot this year, which helps to calm both his and my nerves. Although I am not really a tense person, I do get a little nervous even for a small competition if we have not been out for a while. My trainer knows exactly what to say to relax me if she thinks tension is creeping in.

My daily routine

Our farm Riverdale Equestrian Centre is in The Bronx area of New York city, where I juggle home, kids and horses. I'll drop my children off at school on the way to the stables and then I normally ride four horses. I teach until three in the afternoon and then dash back to collect my children from school which often entails staying late to support their sporting efforts in basketball and hockey. During my dressage competition season, from January to April, Poppy and I go down to Florida to compete and train on the weekends, then I fly back to New York for a couple of days then fly back to Florida. Evi Pracht, my trainer, escapes from the cold Canadian winter weather and comes to Florida to help me. Evi is my eyes on the ground and these training sessions are very important to me. In New York my training is not so consistent, I don't have the luxury of regular help and I get people to watch me when they can. Robert Dover has been a great help when he is in New York.

Besides riding, I keep fit by running and I also love water skiing, which I do when I am in Florida, as well as in the summer, at a lake near our house. When I was younger, growing up in Canada, I did a lot of downhill ski racing, now I only ski for fun and fitness. I know I am lucky that I have a husband who is so supportive of me. Rusty was an International show jumper himself, placing 2nd at the World Equestrian Games in 1990 and representing the United States at the Barcelona Olympics in 1992. We met at the Pan American Games in Havana and that was that, now married and two children later, my home is in the United States but I still ride for Canada. He understands my life and is my biggest supporter together with my children - I couldn't ask for a better cheering squad.

How my riding career began

As a child I spent most of my summers in Scotland, as both of my parents were born there. When I was 10, my mum made the fatal mistake of buying me the book 'Jill Goes Pony Trekking in Edinburgh' and I remember saying to her 'Please can we try it!' There were stables in the middle of Toronto, where I grew up, called Sunnybrook stables, so when we got back after the summer holidays, my mother called them. I managed to convince my brother, my best friend and her brother to take lessons with me. But I was the only one that got hooked, the rest of them never tried it again. After that there was no stopping me, I continually harassed my parents for my own horse until one Christmas morning when I was given a huge framed card saying 'IOU one horse'. As neither of my parents knew anything about horses, we relied on a riding instructor friend of my mother's to help us find Gloria, my first horse. I had Gloria for seven years and although she was nothing to write home about, she was certainly the most special horse to me and together we did our first dressage test.

When I was eighteen I trained with Ginny Sinclair. Her father was head of what we now call Dressage Canada. Don Sinclair was organising funding for a

My Competition Highlights

1981 Bronze medal at NA Young Riders Championships.

1986 Attended World Dressage Championships in Canada on Orsk.

1988 Team Bronze Seoul Olympics on Reipo.

1989 6th at World Cup Finals Stockholm Sweden on Reipo.

1991 Team Gold at the Pan American Games Havana Cuba on Kronjuwel.

1998 1st Grand Prix and Special Florida Dressage Classic, 3rd Grand Prix at CDI-W Loxahatchee Florida on Imperioso.

2002 Individual Silver FEI Coupes des Ameriques Quebec on Imperioso.

2003 Team Silver at the Pan American Games Santo Domingo, Dominican Republic on Gambol.

2004 Member of the Canadian Olympic team in Athens on Imperioso.

2005 1st Grand Prix and Freestyle Washington International Dressage Championships on Gambol, 1st Grand Prix and Freestyle CDI3* Saugerties New England on Imperioso.

2006 1st and 2nd FEI Grand Prix CDN Wellington Florida on Imperioso and Gambol respectively, 1st Grand Prix Kur on Gambol, 3rd FEI Grand Prix and 1st Grand Prix Kur on Gambol, 3rd FEI Grand Prix on Imperioso CDI Florida Dressage Classic, 2nd FEI CDI-W Grand Prix Special WEF Dressage Classic Florida on Imperioso.

selection of young riders who showed talent in dressage to train in Europe. I couldn't believe that I was chosen to spend three years in Germany training with Johann Hinnemann and then later with Willi Schultheiss. I don't know if I would have the career I have today in dressage without the financial support Mr. Sinclair organised back then. Success isn't only about hard work, it is also about taking full advantage of those opportunities that come your way and making the most of them.

My ambition is now to experience the World Equestrian Games in Kentucky on Poppy. I think it would be just fantastic to compete so close to home at such a prestigious event. And of course, there are the Olympics coming up in London, at which my children desperately want me to compete, as they will have all their Scottish cousins to join in supporting me.

Evi Pracht

The Trainer

Above *Evi Pracht, who has been Ashley's trainer for almost 25 years, attending the CHIO at Aachen 2009*
Opposite *Evi and Ashley on the podium, along with team mates Cynthia Neale and Gina Smith, receiving the Bronze medal for Canada at the Seoul Olympics in 1988. This is the only Olympic medal that Canada has won in dressage*

My Story

1937 I was born Eva Maria Neckermann on June 29th in Wuzburg Germany.

1953 Under the supervision of my father Joseph Neckerman I began riding when I was 16, with further training under Bubi Gunther, Willi Schultheiss and Heinz Lammers.

1974 For the Royal Winter Fair in Toronto, I organised and performed a dressage Pas de Trois demonstration on three white horses brought from Germany.

1981 We moved to Cedar Valley Ontario Canada.

1986 We hosted the World Championships at our barn in Ontario, Canada, the first time this competition was held outside Europe.

Training Ashley and Pop Art

I have known Ashley a very long time. We first met when she was training in Germany with Johann Hinnemann and Willi Schultheiss, then when I moved to Canada in 1981, Ashley came to ride at our stables in Cedar Valley, north of Toronto. She was a talented young rider with lots of passion and always willing to work hard. I could tell right from the beginning that she would do well. Later in 1988 we were teammates on the Canadian Olympic team that went to Seoul. We won the first and only Olympic medal for Canada in dressage. Ashley is such a good friend to me and there is nothing I would not do for her.

I go to Florida during the winter show season from January until April. Ashley competes there and I help her from the ground some days. It also gives me the opportunity to attend her most important competitions. Ashley is so experienced and her relationship with Pop Art very settled now, that the rest of the year when she is in New York, I only fly out to help her if she has a really important competition coming up or if she feels she needs my help. From my days as a Grand Prix rider in Germany and Canada, I believe the rider always needs someone on the ground to point out the little things that can be done better and I give her some tips which I remember from my riding career. This is how I help Ashley and Pop Art. She knows when the horse is supple enough and how to warm him up, my job is to point out when maybe the pirouette is too big and I'll say do you want a 9 or a 7? Or maybe the hind leg is not jumping well enough, or perhaps there could be a little more extension in the extended trot, in which case I'll tell Ashley 'come on be brave'. Communication goes both ways with us and it is very productive to be able to sit down and discuss your strengths and weaknesses and the direction the training is taking.

Although Poppy's paces are all fantastic we have had to work a little on his halt, so that he really is square, and on his extended trot to make it even more spectacular. But his piaffe and passage transitions are his forte. I must admit I have never seen a horse with a piaffe and passage as good as Pop Art's. In Ashley's kur, she does movements which I don't think the judges realise the difficulty of, as Pop Art does them so easily, for example the piaffe-pirouette where Ashley turns him to the left and right without moving from the spot then down the centre line, and two double canter pirouettes within twenty metres. Poppy is such a wonderful, pleasant horse, I just love him, and he is such a good friend to Ashley he really tries so hard for her. Most often you get a horse where one of the basic paces could be better, but all three of Pop Art's paces are fantastic, which is just as well, because I don't believe you can 'fix' a bad canter to a 100%.

I have always been crazy about horses since the day I could talk. I remember in Germany in 1947 when I was 8, after the War, for my First Holy Communion, my father, Josef Neckermann, arranged for a horse drawn carriage to take me to Church and that was the best present ever. After the ceremony I was allowed to sit on one of the horses in my white confirmation dress. I loved it and really didn't want to get off, even though the horse went wild, as it was not used to being ridden. My father rode horses as a young boy but due to his education and work commitments had given it up for more than 24 years. But after I begged him to start riding again, he took it back up in 1950 and represented Germany at four different Olympic Games winning two Gold medals, two Silver medals and two Bronze medals.

I didn't start riding properly until I was sixteen, under my father's instruction. He was really the strictest teacher ever, he was such a perfectionist. I also trained under Willi Schultheiss and Bubi Gunther. When I made the German National team, they asked me to choose between Show-jumping and Dressage, as I was competing Grand Prix in both disciplines. At that time I had a super little stallion, but he couldn't jump at all. I couldn't bear to give him up so I decided to focus on improving my dressage.

My husband, Hans Pracht was a successful showjumper and businessman and together we ran our stables in Germany. In the early '70s, we were invited to perform a Pas de Trois at the Royal Winter Fair in Toronto. We fell in love with Canada and after several visits, including the warm-up competition for the Montreal Olympics in 1976, we immigrated there in 1981. We built lovely stables in Cedar Valley called International Equestrian Sport Services where we have held many international competitions including the

Evi's Competition Highlights

1969 14th Grand Prix at European Champions at Wolfsburg (FRG) on Antoinette.

1974 1st Grand Prix at CDI Goodwood on Van Eick, 1st Prix St Georges and Intermediaire I at Goodwood on Duccas.

1982 Member of the Canadian World Championship Team in Lausanne.

1984 Canadian Dressage Team competing at the Los Angeles Olympics on Little Joe.

1987 Individual Silver and Team Gold Pan American Games on Emirage

1988 Team Bronze Seoul Olympic Games on Emirage - the only medal ever won by the Canadian team.

1990 World Cup Final at 's Hertogenbosch.

1986 World Championships which was the first time this competition was held outside Europe. I competed for Canada at the Pan American Games, two Olympics and World Cup Finals on my horse called Emirage. My daughter, Martina, has also become a very successful international rider competing for Canada in the Young Rider division through to the Pan Am games and the Olympics, often riding Emirage.

Nowadays I don't really ride. I love teaching and I can focus on my grand-daughter who is showing the family passion for riding and of course I have Ashley.

My horses were always my best friends, and it is my opinion that for success in the ring, your horse must truly be a good friend. That is what Ashley and Pop Art have, not only are they talented athletes but they are very, very good friends.

Above *Pop Art or 'Poppy' as he is known to his friends*
Opposite, left *Ashley and Poppy doing tempi changes*
Opposite, right *Ashley and Poppy receiving their 5th place rosette and congratulations from the judges and sponsors of the World Dressage Masters Grand Prix Kur held at Hickstead 2009*

Pop Art
The Horse

A day in the life

Pop Art or Poppy, as we call him at home, is a Dutch Warmblood gelding. I am really lucky I found him as it was just by chance I even tried him out. Sjef Janssen was helping me find a horse in Holland. We were in a hurry but heard this particular stable had a few interesting horses. The first one I rode threw me off so we were just going to leave and not try the others, but they already had this lovely chestnut gelding tacked up and ready. He was beautiful and went so well and this was Poppy. He is such a great animal and, as he is so sweet, he is more of a family pet than horse, especially to my children. He is also quite a character and likes to grab the broom when I am sweeping in the yard to try his hand at sweeping.

I believe that horses should have as normal a horse life as possible. Poppy gets hand walked for about 15 - 20 minutes each day before I ride him, which I tend to do first thing in the morning. I try not to overwork him, always giving him little walk breaks to let the muscles recharge and then repeating the exercise. If I need to work on something I try not to go overboard on it. After being ridden he goes back to his stable for some hay and then a little later he'll go out in the paddock for about five hours each day.

Poppy loves other horses but sadly he lost a great stable friend in 2007, when my stallion Imperioso died. Poppy and Perry were such good friends, I often found them grooming each other over the stable door as they had adjacent stables.

He really is just like a normal horse, but he just happens to be very good at what he does. In fact he was tremendous at Prix St Georges tests, he was never beaten, we won absolutely everything. At shows I try to keep his routine as close to what he does at home. I think that is where things went wrong at the Olympics in Hong Kong, because his routine had to change drastically due to the long journey to get there, hot weather, time-zone changes and, of course, quarantine. Often there was no turnout for him so he had a lot of

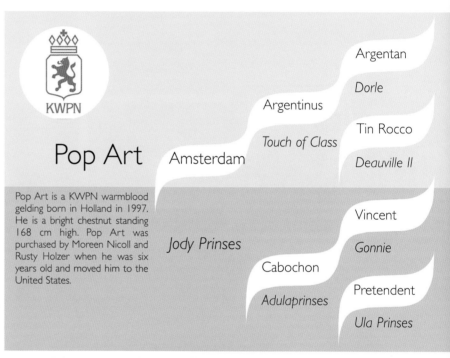

Pop Art's Competition Highlights

2006 1st Prix St Georges, Intermediare I and 1st Intermediare Freestyle WEF Dressage Classic CDI3 Florida; 1st Prix St Georges, Intermediare I and 1st Intermediare Freestyle Gold Coast Opener Festival CDI3.

2007 1st Grand Prix FEI CDN Wellington Florida, 1st Grand Prix and 1st Grand Prix Kur CDI Loxahatchee Florida, 1st Grand Prix and 1st Grand Prix Kur CDI-W Saugerties USA, 3rd

Grand Prix Kur CDI Devon USA

2008 1st Grand Prix and 1st Grand Prix Kur CDI-W Palm Beach Dressage Derby Florida, 1st Grand Prix and 1st Grand Prix Kur CDI Wellington Florida.

2009 1st Grand Prix and Kur CDI-W Gold Coast Opener Palm Beach Florida, 2nd Grand Prix and 4th Kur CDI World Dressage Masters Palm Beach Florida, 5th Grand Prix and Kur World Cup Finals Las Vegas, 5th Grand Prix, 5th Kur World Dressage Masters at Hickstead, United Kingdom.

KWPN

Pop Art

Amsterdam

Argentinus

Touch of Class

Argentan

Dorle

Tin Rocco

Deauville II

Jody Prinses

Cabochon

Adulaprinses

Vincent

Gonnie

Pretendent

Ula Prinses

Pop Art is a KWPN warmblood gelding born in Holland in 1997. He is a bright chestnut standing 168 cm high. Pop Art was purchased by Moreen Nicoll and Rusty Holzer when he was six years old and moved him to the United States.

routine adjustments to make which affected his performance. When I am in America it is easier to keep to our daily schedule as I can ship him in literally the day before the competition, so that he can still be turned out and stick to his routine. Recently I have had more success with this strategy. In fact, so far this competitive season, he has felt so easy that it has been great fun to ride and compete him.

Unlike Europe where riding is a way of life for many people, to own horses in America and particularly to own a farm in the middle of New York City is quite unusual and considered to be very elitist. But this attitude towards horse sports is beginning to change slowly as more Americans are riding for fun now. This increase in participation will encourage more sponsors and businesses to get involved when they realise the benefits of advertising as audience numbers increase at the big events. All of this will help draw attention to the sport so we can start to develop a broader base of riders and horses to choose our International Squads from. We have a long way to go to catch up with the Europeans. We need more horses like Poppy to do well against their International counterparts, bringing pride to their country, attracting media attention and showing everyone how special they really are.

Ashley Holzer and Pop Art

To take part in this leg of the World Dressage Masters competition held at Hickstead, Ashley and Pop Art flew all the way from New York to England. Pop Art did not let Ashley down, placing 5th in the Grand Prix and 5th again in the Grand Prix Kur. The competition was very stiff with riders coming from Germany, Holland, Poland, Denmark, Portugal and the United States.

The World Dressage Masters is a series of 5 star Grand Prix events held at Palm Beach USA, Salzburg Austria, Munich Germany, Hickstead and Cannes France. Invited rider and horse combinations compete for large purses.

EXQUIS WORLD DRESSAGE MASTERS ©
★★★★★

The World Dressage Masters *is a new sports and marketing concept in dressage. Its goal is to combine top sport, top events and top prize money to help dressage develop to an even more attractive and understandable spectacle. The organisers aim is to increase the popularity and standard of dressage events by showcasing the top riders and horses in the best venues with the belief that by raising the profile and visability of dressage around the world will help to stimulate the sport. Much of the proceeds raised by the World Dressage Masters goes to JustWorld International, a non-profit organisation dedicated to improving the lives of disadvantaged children in the developing world.*

FEI Ponies

The FEI stipulates that ponies competing under FEI rules must not exceed 148 cm, at the withers, without shoes and 149cm with shoes, a 2 cm tolerance margin is applied. Ponies must only be ridden at competitions by a child between the ages of 12 and 16 years old. Ponies must be at least six years old or older.

The first Pony European Dressage competition took place in 1978 in which team Sweden won the Gold medal. For the next four years until 1981 only the team event was held and Sweden took the Gold medals home each time. 1982 saw the Individual competition added along side the Team Test. It was not long before Germany established itself as the nation to beat. From 1982 to 2009 Germany won the Team Gold medal twenty-six times and took home the Individual Gold medal on eighteen occasions. Holland declared themselves the second nation to beat but in terms of medals won they were well behind the consistent German pony riders and purpose bred ponies.

The following chapters are an insight into the lives of some the most promising and successful young pony riders, their trainers and ponies. Unlike the senior professional riders whose main occupation and income source may stem from riding, successful children who ride ponies do so not only because of their riding talent and ability but also because they have the emotional and financial support from their families. Without this backup it just would not be possible for children to compete at this high level as it takes considerable effort to make it onto the National squads.

Most National Federations hold viewing days for 'hopeful' pony squad combinations early in the competitive season. The fortunate children who make the long-list are expected to attend training sessions and to compete at designated selections trials throughout the season where the selectors monitor their progress. These competitions are normally FEI International events, which can run over four days from trot-up to the final Kur. The results from these competitions along with the child's and pony's suitability to training and becoming part of a team are instrumental in the selectors final decision as to who will represent their country at the Pony European Championships.

Pony Shoulder-In

Sönke Rothenberger and Deinhard B

The regularity and fluency of the trot steps remain the same before, during and after the exercise. The pony adopts a uniform bend away from the direction in which it is moving. The shoulders are taken in from the track to an angle of approximately thirty degrees with the hindquarters remaining in the track. Shoulder-in, if performed in the right way, with the pony correctly bent around the inside leg of the rider, and at the correct angle, is not only a suppling exercise but a collecting exercise, because the pony, at every step, must move his inside hind leg underneath his body and place it in front of the outside hind leg, while lowering his inside hip.

Here we see one of the most successful ponies on the circuit with his highly talented rider Sönke Rothenburger. This young man shows an ability in his riding that is almost beyond his years. Not really surprising as he comes from one of the most experienced and successful 'Dressage families' of recent times. Nevertheless, it is quite extraordinary to witness such mature riding ability in one so young.

From this picture it is easy to see the correct and uniform bend of the pony with the acceptance of the controlling outside rein and the light submissive flexion away from the direction in which they are moving. Most impressive of all is to note the absolute balance of both pony and rider, to see the inside hind leg of the pony stepping so perfectly under the centre of balance, thereby enabling him to move with ease and fluency, without any disturbance to the rhythm or cadence of the collected trot itself, giving the impression of effortless power.

Even though, for perfection, the rider is perhaps sitting a little to the outside, his 'feel' and effectiveness allows the harmony of the movement to shine through. This stunning combination have been on the pony cir-cuit for a number of years now and have established a solid, harmonious and impressive partnership. Sönke took over the ride of Deinhard B from Anna von Negri, who, with Deinhard, won the Pony European Dressage Championships in Italy at Pratoni del Vivaro in 2005. Deinhard B has continued establishing himself as a dressage champion under Sönke, with the partnership producing many European Gold and Silver medals. They are trained by Sönke's parents, Sven and Gonnelien Rothenberger who accompany them to every show to provide support and help for the young combination, as well as being successful International dressage riders in their own right. Both are former Olympians, having successfully competed for the Dutch team and winning Team Silver in the 1996 Atlanta Olympics.

The Rothenberger family is, without doubt, one of the most successful 'Dressage families' in Germany, with Sönke's older sister, Sanneke, having produced many victories in her time in Ponies and now Junior level. It is remarkable to see this family unit working together as a team to produce such wonderful horses, riders and ultimately performances.

Sönke Rothenberger

The Rider

My most memorable test

When I was eleven years old and Deinhard was only seven, Mrs Endres, the German Bundestrainer, nominated me to represent my country at the Pony FEI competition in Saumur. This was such a big honour for me, as it was the first time I had competed Deinhard for my country. In the Pony Team Championship Test we placed 3rd with a score of 72.316%. Deinhard was supple and loose and he did everything for me. I felt very relieved at the end of the competition in that I had fulfilled all expectations and perhaps a little bit more.

My daily routine

I was born in Frankfurt on 14th of October 1994, so much of my day is taken up going to school from 8am to 3:15pm. I love to skateboard with my friends so often I will spend another two hours with them before heading home to ride Deinhard, Wolke Sieben, my junior dressage horse and sometimes my jumping horse, Mauna Kea. I have already competed and won some big international classes on my dressage horse, Wolke and in 2008, when I was 14 years old, Wolke and I placed 4th in the Junior Rider classes at the German Championships.

   I think it is important to have other interests and at the moment I breed chickens with my club and I also love to snowboard. If my studies become too much I may have to cut back on riding but if there is the time I

Above *Sönke Rothenberger receiving the Individual Gold medal at the European Pony Championships 2008 held at Avenches, Switzerland*
Opposite, right *Sönke Rothenberger on the podium with the other European Pony Champions, l. to r. Antoinette te Riele on Golden Girl from Holland, Silver medal, Elin Aspnas on Tim from Sweden. Tim and Elin were later eliminated for failing a drugs test*

Sönke's Competition Highlights

2006 5th Pony Team Test, 5th Pony Test D-ZII on Wimbledon at CDNP Weert, 2nd Pony Preliminary and Team Test, 6th Individual Test at CDI-PJYR Stadl Paura, Austria, 3rd Hessian PDB Qualifier Test 1, 4th Test 2 at Preis der Besten, 2nd Pony Team Test, 5th Individual Test at CDN Weert on Wimbledon.

2007 6th Pony Team and Individual Test at CDIO-PJYR Neubeeren, Ger.

2008 1st Pony riders L Test on Wimbledon, 1st Junior Team Test, 3rd Junior Individual Test, 2nd Junior Kur at CDI-PJYR Bonn on Wolke Sieben, 4th and 3rd German Qualifier at CDI Neubeeren, 5th Round 1, 2 and Final at Preis der Besten, Warendorf on Wimbledon.

will always ride and maybe jump as well. My father was successful combining his riding career together with his work and I hope to do the same.

How my riding career began

Both of my parents are active Grand Prix competitors and my older sister is also a successful young rider and my grandparents on both my mother's and father's side also have businesses involving horses, so it would seem likely that I would also ride, but I ride and compete because I love it. My parents have always ensured that we have had good ponies and horses to learn on and to compete on. Deinhard is so talented with his gaits, in my opinion, he could easily be an Olympic champion, if he was a horse. When he was five, he won the Silver medal for dressage ponies at the Bundeschampionate, with scores of 9 from the judges for his basic paces. For some reason I have always preferred to ride stallions and I seem to get on well with Deinhard. To compete at the level Deinhard and I compete at is not so difficult but you do have to be very consistent in your training routine. When I am away competing, I try to keep to my same training system that I use at home. I feel this is important to keep me and Deinhard relaxed. Before my test and my warm-up, I sit in the corner of the tackroom and think about my test. Sometimes I find an area about one metre by two meters to walk the test and think about what I would do when riding Deinhard. I spend a lot of time with Deinhard, grooming him and taking him out for grass but plaiting is one of the things I am not very good at. My parents always accompany me at the shows, I rely on their vast show experience as it protects me from making big mistakes.

Sven Rothenberger

The Trainer

Above *Sven Rothenberger in his role as coach and mentor for his son, Sönke Rothenberger*
Opposite, top *Sönke and Sven walking together from the stables to the main arena for a training session*
Opposite, bottom *The final warm-up before Sönke and Deinhard B enter the arena to do their Gold medal winning Individual test at the European Pony Championships*

My Story

1966 I was born 1 June in Frankfurt am Main

1974 My sister and I began riding school ponies.

1990 I met Gonnelien Gordijn who became my wife.

1991 Adiamo and I were the winners of the first ever Kur at the European Championships.

1996 Gonnelien and I were the first husband and wife team to win a medal together in an Olympic event.

1997 Both Gonnelien and myself rode for Holland at the European Championships where together we won Team Silver. We moved to Gestüt Erlenhof, a family concern, and took over the management of the dressage division.

Training Sönke and Deinhard B

I suppose the secret to my success, as a rider and then trainer, is my belief that one should adapt to the horse rather than the other way around. When I decide to buy a more established horse it is because I see how well they move and perhaps I see more potential in them to do even better. This is a credit to the trainer of that horse and I would buy the horse to do better, not to undo their training, just to start over again. This is why I have been able to do very well in the Grand Prix, after owning a horse for only a few days, such as was the case with Weyden. I bought Weyden after seeing him only three times. He was such a natural moving horse. The owner wrote out his instructions on how to handle him and I followed his advice rather than impose my own ways on him. Within a few months Weyden was on the Olympic Team after winning several Grand Prix competitions with me. This is a principle I would like to instil in my own children as they learn dressage and learn about their ponies and horses - that riding is a partnership and the rider must be good enough to adapt his riding to the way of the horse.

Although I spend most of my day working in business, I am still passionate about dressage and compete when I can and, particularly now that my children have taken up the sport, I can get involved at many different levels. My son Sönke and I will work together about two times a week. The other times my wife, Gonnelien and our trainer, Herr Heinz-Günther Scholten take over but I like to feel that my experiences and wisdom can benefit Sönke and Deinhard B. Sönke and I are also very close so it is sometimes a positive experience when Herr Scholten can step in to make the corrections. My relationship with Sönke, as his trainer, is good but it can undeniably be difficult when things are not going well because I am also his father. When he is having success then it is ok. At shows I am always on hand and often all three of us, Gonnelien, Herr Scholten and myself are there to help Sönke in the warm-up before the competition.

During the warm up at competitions we work together on movements which he needs to improve on the most, such as the transitions to walk and back to canter again. The last five minutes before Sönke and Deinhard B enter the arena, Sönke likes to work on his own. He knows what Deinhard needs to do to perform a good test and this gives him a moment to collect his thoughts.

Sven's Competition Highlights

1990 1st World Cup Final in 's Hertogenbosch on Andiamo, Team Gold WEG Stockholm on Ideaal.

1991 Team (Ger) and Individual Gold at European Championships in Germany, 1st Grand Prix and Kur at Goodwood, UK on Andiamo.

1992 2nd World Cup Final on Ideaal.

1993 Silver (Ger) Individual and Kur at European Championships in Slovenia on Andiamo, 2nd World Cup Final on Ideaal.

1995 Team Silver (NL) and Individual Bronze at European Championships in Luxembourg on Olympic Bo.

1996 Team Silver, Individual Bronze at Atlanta Olympics on Weyden.

1997 1st CDI of Neumunster Team

Silver (NL) at European Championships in Germany, 2nd World Cup Final on Jonggor's Weyden.

1998 4th Dutch Dressage Championships on Without a Doubt.

1999 1st Grand Prix, 3rd Special, 3rd Kur Dutch National Championships on Jonggor's Weyden.

2003 10th Grand Prix, 6th Kur at CDI Berlin, 9th Grand Prix, 5th Kur at CDI-W Maastricht, 6th Grand Prix and Kur at CDIO Mondorf Les Bains on Barclay II

2004 7th Grand Prix, 8th Kur at CDI-W Maastricht, 3rd Grand Prix, 5th Kur CDI-W 's Hertogenbosch, 7th Grand Prix and Kur at CDI-W Amsterdam, Team 4th, Individual 17th at Athens Olympics on Barclay II.

2005 7th Grand Prix and Kur at CDI-W Dusseldorf, Team Bronze European Championships at Hagen on Barclay II.

Deinhard B

The Pony

Above *Sven Rothenberger acting as groom for his son while his son stands on the podium to receive the Gold medal for the Individual Test at the European Pony Championships. The Rothenberger family are very successful horse people with both parents competing at Grand Prix level and Sönke's older sister, Sanneke having won numerous Gold medals in the Pony and Junior Rider divisions. Both parents attend the competitions their children participate in and they play an active role in coaching and grooming to ensure that their children and their ponies are well cared for*

I first saw Deinhard B in the winter of 2005 when he was just six years old. I liked him instantly as he was so beautiful and charming. In my opinion he was the best pony I have ever seen. We were very lucky to buy him just before he became successful in May at the CDIP in Saumur where he was placed high. Shortly after we bought him, he won the Preis der Besten and also won the Gold medal at the Pony European Championships in Italy, with a young German rider, Anna von Negri. Anna has won many pony competitions riding several different ponies and it was good that she was able to ride Deinhard for us in his first competitive year.

When I first started to compete I had always wanted to ride a stallion. At the time there were not many opportunities to find a good quality pony, that was also a stallion. We knew Deinhard was not going to be so easy to ride but my parents felt that I had the talent to cope with him. I had shown them previously with another pony, Wimbledon that I was competing before we got Deinhard, that I was good enough to manage a pony at this international level.

At home we call him Deini and every morning his groom puts him on the horse walker for half an hour and then afterwards, if it is the winter he goes into a sand paddock or if it is summer, he goes onto a grass paddock. Most days I ride him in the afternoon. Deini knows that he is a champion and he expects to be treated as one - which I think he is.

Deinhard already has produced some very nice sons and daughters, but at the moment we are concentrating more on his competitive career. When I am 16 and move onto horses we had planned that my younger sister will continue to ride and compete him. They are both 10 years old. After my sister has finished riding ponies we will organise a breeding career for him.

I am hoping that the transition onto horses will not be too much of a jump as Deinhard's paces are so big it is already like riding a horse. Although I have another year on him I have already been competing in some Junior classes on my new horse.

Deinhard B's Competition Highlights

2003 4th Riding Pony Stallion division at Bundeschampionships.

2004 2nd Riding Pony Stallion division at Bundeschampionships, ridden by Anna von Negri.

2005 2nd Bundeschampionships ridden by Anna von Negri, 1st Preis der Besten, 1st CDIP Saumur France, 4th Preliminary Test, 2nd Team Championship Test, 3rd Individual Finals at CDIP Freudenberg, Team Gold and Individual Gold European Pony Championships Italy, ridden by Anna von Negri, 8th Pony Team Test at CDN Weert with Sönke Rothenberger.

2006 4th CDIP Weikersdorf Austria, 4th Pony Team Test, 3rd Pony Test D-ZII CDNP Weert Netherlands, 3rd Team Championships Saumur, 10th German Youth Championships, 7th Pony Preliminary Test CDI-PJYR Stadl Paura Austria, 4th Hessian PDB Test 1 at Preis der Besten ridden by Sönke Rothenberger.

2007 Team Gold, Individual Bronze European Pony Championships Freudenberg Germany, 4th German Youth Championships, 4th Pony Team Test, 3rd Individual Test at CDIO-PJYR Neubeeren, 2nd Preliminary and Individual Tests and 4th Team at CDIP Bonn ridden by Sönke Rothenberger.

2008 Team Bronze and 4th Individual at CDIP Addington UK, 2nd Preis der Besten, 1st CDIP in Pony Preliminary Test, Team Championship Test and Individual Test at Bonn, Germany, 1st CDIO Neubeeren, Germany, Team Gold and Individual Gold at European Pony Championships Switzerland ridden by Sönke Rothenberger.

2009 1st Round One, 1st Round Two, 1st Preis der Besten, 1st Individual Test and Kur at CDI Bonn, Team Gold European Pony Championships Moorsele ridden by Sönke Rothenberger.

Deinhard B

Deinhard B is a palomino Rhinelander stallion born in 1999. He was bred by Ludwig Stassen of Gestüt Bonninger in Germany. In 2005 Deinhard B was bought by the Rothenberger family with the intention that he would be ridden by Sönke.

Dornik B	Derano Gold	Derano
		Viktoria
	Dubary	Derbino
		Vienna
Gwenduline B	Golden Dancer	Dancer
		Golden Charm
	Gioconda	Goldstrand
		Waldfee

Above *An excited Deinhard B and Sönke on their victory lap after receiving the Individual Gold medal*

Left *Sönke who rode for the German Pony Squad followed by his cousin Antoinette te Riele on Golden Girl who rode for the Dutch Pony Squad having just received Gold and Silver medals respectfully at the European Pony Championships 2008*

Pony Collected Canter

Katharina Weychert and Dornik B

The pony, remaining 'on the bit', moves forward with cadence and the neck is raised and arched. The hocks, being well engaged, maintain an energetic impulsion, enabling the shoulders to move with greater mobility, thus demonstrating self-carriage and an uphill tendency. The pony's strides are shorter than in the other canters without losing elasticity and cadence.

Dornik B is one of the most successful ponies to have competed in recent years and to think that he has a breeding career to match. Seen here with his very accomplished rider, Katharina Weychert in the collected canter, they make a wonderful picture of harmony and togetherness. The rapport they have managed to mould between each other is certainly a pleasure to watch. Katharina is the last competitive partner Dornik B will have, as he was retired from the show ring this year to enjoy his life at the Bonniger Stud in Germany where he was born.

To see his highly engaged hindquarters with his inside leg stepping so well underneath his body weight, with the energy enabling the shoulders to be so light and mobile that it makes it so easy for his rider to direct him through all of the canter exercises with great confidence and fluency, makes the whole picture very 'easy on the eye.' The elasticity and cadence this 18 year old master still possesses is a testament to the good management and care he has received all his life.

We can see the beginning of the true canter sequence with the outside (right) hind leg starting the motion, the outside diagonal (right fore and left hind) about to reach the ground simultaneously, and then finally the inside (left) fore finishing the 'three time beat' of the canter sequence, with all joints correctly bent, emphasizing the expression of the canter itself. Following this

will be the moment of suspension and then the whole 'three time' sequence will begin again.

His elegant rider is sitting well in the saddle with good balance and a deep supple seat, perhaps the hands are carried a little high, but the contact is light and forwards and is in no way supporting or restricting the pony's frame.

To have the opportunity to ride a pony of this calibre at such a young age is every young rider's dream but only a few will have the experience. To find such a well bred pony who possesses the high quality movements naturally and then to have an experienced small rider to patiently, skillfuly train the pony to FEI pony standards is a feat in itself. Added to this one must then find a tactful knowledgeable trainer who can relay these techniques to a young child of between 12 and 16 so they can ask the pony to perform at his best is a very tall order indeed and one that is not achieved by many.

Katharina has taken advantage of this amazing opportunity to learn all that she can from Dornik B before moving on to horses as did Dornik B's other young child riders who are now enjoying successful Junior and Young Rider careers. Dornik B has now returned to the Bonniger Stud, the place of his birth and is enjoying his well deserved retirement from the showring. He will continue his breeding duties as he is a stallion much in demand amongst serious pony breeders.

Katharina Weychert

The Rider

My daily routine

We don't live on a farm so our horses are stabled about 50km away in the Bavarian district. We have a groom who lives at the stables and looks after our horses and ponies for us. I leave to ride Dornik and my other pony, Golden Derano C, about 3pm everyday, often having to do my homework in the car as we travel. My trainer, Mr Heinz-Günther Scholten, comes to help me two or three times each week and, of course, there are the lessons with Mrs Endres. I ride on my own the rest of the time. In the winter I must be very disciplined as I have to work on my own even more. We met Mr Scholten when we bought Golden Derano in the spring of 2006 as he was Derano's trainer. We were very pleased with how Derano was going, so we asked Mr. Scholten if he would continue training with us and when we got Dornik, he began helping us with him as well. I ride every day so there is little time for other things - not that I mind.

At competitions my whole family comes to help out along with our groom, Madeleine. There are so many competitions that Dornik and I need to attend and without my family's support, it would not be possible to

Katharina's Competition Highlights

2007 5th Pony Riders at German Youth Championships on Golden Derano C.

2008 8th Preis der Besten, 2nd and 1st Pony L Test at CDIP Bonn, 4th German Qualifier at CDN Neubeeren, 1st Pony Preliminary Team and Individual Tests at CDIP Babenhausen on Golden Derano.

2009 1st Test 1 2nd Test 2 at Preis der Besten qualifier, 5th round 1 10th round 2 8th Final at Preis der Besten, 1st Team Test at CDI-PJYR Moorsele, Belgium on Golden Derano C, Team Gold 7th Individually, Individual Bronze medal Silver medal Kur at Pony European Championships at Moorsele, Belgium.

ride at this level on such a good pony as Dornik. Dornik loves the travelling and competitions - at shows he is very relaxed and easy to handle. During our warm up I try to concentrate on keeping him relaxed and elastic. I can tell when Dornik is going to fight for me and do his best. When he is like this we can enter the arena in a good frame of mind

How my riding career began

My father was a great showjumping competitor at the Nation's Cup level years ago, so I think I developed an interest in riding from him. Like most children I started on a very small pony. He was called Billie. Billie is now very old but we still keep him as he is great company for the other ponies we own. Dornik B goes out in the field with Billie every day. I also have two younger sisters who are interested in riding so Billie will still get lots of attention. I am very ambitious when it comes to riding and I intend to continue competing in the Junior division when I turn 17. I already have a horse in mind that I would like to train on.

Opposite, main picture *Katharina Weychert on the podium to receive her Team Gold medal at the European Pony Championships*
Opposite, bottom *Dornik B in extended trot*
Above, left *Katharina and Dornik B demonstrating airbourne suspension in the extended canter*
Above, right *Katharina and Dornik B receiving their rosette for placing 6th in the Individual Finals at the Pony European Championships*

Above *Heinz-Günther, trainer of many success-ful pony dressage riders*
Opposite *Heinz-Günther training Katharina and Dornik B at the European Pony Championships in the main arena. The organis-ers of FEI events allow competitors to ride in the main arenas at specified times to give them a chance to get used to the arena*

Heinz-Günther Scholten

The Trainer

Training Katharina and Dornik B

I was born in Dusseldorf which is very close to the Bonniger Stud. When I went to visit the stud to meet Mr Bonniger, I also met Dornik B for the first time. Dornik B was only two and a half years old and already he was so balanced. At three, he was a great pony. It was not until Katharina got the ride on Dornik in 2008 that I became involved with his training.

Over the past 20 years I have been involved with the training of many successful Bonniger ponies and their riders. There was Daniela Hintenlang who had the roan pony stallion, Drei B Valerian. Daniela went to the Pony European Championships in 1989. He was fol-lowed by his sister, Nicolle, who won the Gold Individual medal at the Pony European Championships held in Stockholm, Sweden, on Daniela's pony. Nicolle was given a pony to train from Mr Bonniger, which was Derano Gold, the sire of Katharina's other pony Golden Derano C. Two years later Nicolle won the Team Gold and Individual Gold medals on Derano Gold and fol-lowed on the next year by winning the Team Gold and Individual Silver on him. I have been training ponies and pony riders for a very long time.

I now live in South Hessen near Mannheim, Heidelberg. I used to train with Johann Hinnemann, it was a coincidence really, as he lived less than 50km away, but I didn't compete very much - I did most of my riding at home. Many of my clients were young rid-ers or pony riders that required looking after at compe-titions, to do both at the same time, properly, just does-n't work so I gave up the competition side. I enjoy help-ing the young people and working with them. I also have several adult riding clients, so it is a good balance.

I met Katharina when she bought Golden Derano C from the Schaefer family. I trained Kaja Schaefer and Golden Derano C while Kaja was on the German pony squad. Since I knew the pony so well, Katharina want-

ed me to continue to train both of them and then Dornik B arrived so I worked with him as well.

Dornik is such a good schoolmaster. He doesn't have to learn anything new anymore. He can do everything so easily, he is very clever. The thing is to keep him supple and in a good mood. You only need to polish up the details before a competition.

Katharina is a very determined girl. She has her goals and is very ambitious. You have to be so hard-working to ride alongside going to school. School gets more and more demanding from year to year and then not just one pony, but two ponies, to work, requires good time management and industriousness. Sacrifices have to be made, such as meeting up with friends and Katharina is happy to make these sacrifices.

Good riders are not born. My experience over the last 20 years, is to start a child riding as early as possible at around the age of seven, eight or nine and focus on developing the seat. Make sure the child has a pony which is suitable for their age. One that is good through the back and in its mouth and does not have any problems in the poll, so that the child can really benefit. If a child has a bad pony and learns the incorrect seat and the pony is too naughty so that it throws the rider off - that is a problem. I prefer to get the child right from the beginning, rather than getting an eleven or twelve year old that has done some riding but incorrectly. To correct the problems is a lot more difficult than starting correctly. Also, if you see the children that have moved on to horses from the top ponies they have it much easier compared to someone who starts with horses. These pony kids have so much routine and experience and they know their way around a 20m x 60m arena. Those kids who have just been given a good horse are behind. The proportion of juniors and young riders that have ridden international ponies is very high.

A good pony must possess good paces. But good paces are not enough in the pony world, they must also be able to be ridden by children. There are lots of ponies with fabulous paces that don't listen and are therefore not suitable as a child's mount.

Above *Dornik B, one of Germany's most successful ponies both as a breeding stallion and dressage competition pony, standing at the Bonniger Stud in Tonisvorst, Germany*
Opposite, top *The famous son, Deinhard B, of the famous father. Dornik B has sired many successful offspring, which due to their easy going nature and athletic talent, make excellent riding ponies for children. It is not unusual in Germany to find several Dornik B ponies competing against each other*
Opposite, bottom *Trudie Sens, Dornik B's first trainer and rider, enjoying their victory lap at the Bundeschampionate*

Dornik B

The Pony

A day in the life

Dornik B is now 19 years old and knows how to look after himself. He is the ideal schoolmaster, as he knows all of the pony dressage movements. Sometimes his conservation of energy makes him a bit lazy but his long reliable career as an FEI dressage pony and breeding stallion has made him one of the most successful ponies in Germany. Despite being a stallion, his wonderful temperament makes him very easy and willing to be handled by children. Dornik was bred and raised at the 45 year old Gestüt Bonniger in Tonisvorst, Germany, known for its success worldwide in breeding and producing dressage ponies. The stud, managed by Ludwig Stassen, boasts many Bundeschampionship winners, European Gold medals and German National titles along with countless first place ribbons at CDIPs held throughout Europe - the result of decades of selective breeding and good training. Dornik B was trained and shown initially, as a young stallion, at the Bundeschampionship by Trudie Sens. When Dornik was nine years old he won his first European Gold medal with Marion Englen in the saddle, a feat which they repeated the following year. Dornik was then ridden by Stephanie Jansen who had a successful competition year, culminating in winning the Team Gold medal at the European Championships. He was then ridden for a year by Anna von Negri, again winning the Team and Individual Gold medals at the European Championships. The following three years, he remained with Louisa Luttgen who, in 2007, won the European Gold medal with a record-breaking score of 77.35%, a record previously held by another Bonniger offspring, Golden Dancer. With Louisa turning 16 and no longer able to compete on a pony, the lease for Dornik B was passed onto Katharina Weychert, who brought Dornik to her stables in August 2007. The Bonniger Stud recognise that Dornik has nothing left to prove and could retire to a life of breeding but he loves the children and enjoys the competitive side of his life, so they have allowed him to continue.

As a breeding stallion Dornik's progeny have represented Germany on many European squads. His sons Dornik Double and Deinhard B, both stallions, have competed on European squads with their father. Dornik B will no doubt retire from the show ring in the near future. He leaves behind an enviable competition record and a legacy in breeding that is set to continue. He has sired over 17 licensed sons and 27 state-premium daughters culminating in a long list of Bundeschampions, international FEI ponies and Gold medal premium foals.

Dornik B's Competition Highlights

1994 1st Bundeschampionate 3 year old Stallion with Trudie Sens.

1995 1st Bundeschampionate 4 year old Stallion with Trudie Sens.

1996 1st Bundeschampionate 5 year old Stallion.

1997 1st Bundeschampionate 6 year old Stallion.

2000 1st Pony Preliminary Test, Team Gold, 1st Individual at Pony European Championships with Marion Englen.

2001 1st Pony Preliminary Test, Team Gold, 1st Individual at Pony European Championships with Marion Englen.

2002 3rd Pony Preliminary and Individual Test, Team Gold at Pony European Championships, 1st Preis der Besten at Warendorf with Stephanie Jansen.

2003 3rd Pony German Championships, with Louisa Luttgen.

2004 2nd Pony Preliminary, Team Gold, 1st Individual Test Pony European Championships at Jaszkowo, Poland, 4th Pony Preliminary, Team Gold at CDIO-P Freudenberg, 3rd Preis der Besten Warendorf with Anna von Negri.

2005 Team Gold, 7th Individual at European Pony Championships Italy, 2nd Pony Preliminary, Team Gold, 2nd Pony Kur at CDIO Saumur with Louisa Luttgen.

2006 3rd Pony Preliminary Test, Team Gold, 2nd Individual Pony European Championships France, 3rd Preis der Besten, 1st Individual Test, Team Gold at CDIP Stadl Paura Austria, 1st Preliminary Test, Team Gold 1st Kur at CDIP Aachen with Louisa Luttgen.

2007 1st Pony Preliminary and Individual Test, Team Gold Pony European Championships at Freudenberg, 2nd Preis der Besten, 1st Pony Preliminary, Team and Individual at CDIP Bonn, 1st German Youth Championships with Louisa Luttgen.

2008 2nd Pony Preliminary Test, Team Gold, 6th Individual at Pony European Championships Avenches, 4th Preis der Besten, 2nd Pony Preliminary and Team Tests 4th Individual at CDIP Bonn with Katharina Weychert.

2009 7th Round 1 Preis der Besten with Katharina Weychert. 1st Frankonian Championships with Michaela Weychert.

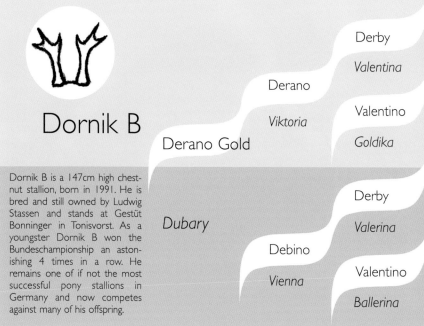

Dornik B

Dornik B is a 147cm high chestnut stallion, born in 1991. He is bred and still owned by Ludwig Stassen and stands at Gestüt Bonninger in Tonisvorst. As a youngster Dornik B won the Bundeschampionship an astonishing 4 times in a row. He remains one of if not the most successful pony stallions in Germany and now competes against many of his offspring.

			Derby
		Derano	Valentina
	Derano Gold	Viktoria	Valentino
Dornik B			Goldika
	Dubary	Debino	Derby
			Valerina
		Vienna	Valentino
			Ballerina

Pony Extended Trot

Carlotta Hassenbürger and Dulcia

The pony covers as much ground as possible, without any loss of regularity or quickening of the tempo. The steps are lengthened to the utmost as a result of great impulsion from the hindquarters. The rider allows the pony to lengthen the frame and to gain ground while controlling the poll. The forefeet should touch the ground on the spot towards which they are pointing. The movement of the fore and hind legs should reach equally forward in the moment of extension. The whole movement should be well balanced, and the transition to collected trot should be smoothly executed by taking more weight on the hindquarters.

Here we see yet another fine example of great riding from one of the sports hopefully 'Top Riders' of the future, Carlotta Hassenbürger, with the lovely palamino mare Dulcia out of Arts Dancer-Boy. This shot of the pair in extended trot captures the impression of Dulcia performing at 'full power' whilst remaining perfectly calm and in superb balance and correct carriage. The energy and thrust from the hindquarters carries her forwards and shows an almost perfect matching of the hind and front legs, with the cannon bone on each limb forming virtually parallel lines. Her carriage is very correct, with the poll remaining the highest part of the neck and the front line of the face being just ahead of the vertical.

The rider is sitting well but, to be super critical, could perhaps be a little more upright with a little more weight coming down the back of her leg and into her heel. However, it is very impressive to see the very clear straight line contact from her elbows through her hands and reins to the pony's mouth. A very promising position indeed for one so young and at the beginning of her FEI career.

This is a very successful pony and rider combination, with the pair coming second individually at the European Pony Championships at Freudenberg, Germany in 2007 and winning the Team Test helping Germany continue their domination of the FEI Pony Dressage. These enviable feats all occurred during Carlotta's first year of riding at FEI Pony level.

Dulcia as a young filly was rumoured to be the pony to watch for the future. Her record breaking results in the Bundeschampionate served only to support this suggestion. Furthermore her transition into FEI Pony level has confirmed Dulcia as one of Germany's most successful FEI ponies with many wins already confirmed and many more to come.

Carlotta comes from a family of keen horse lovers, with her two older brothers being successful showjumpers. It is marvellous to see such a high level of dedication and commitment in one so young. Of course it goes without saying that her achievements would not have been possible if it were not for the help and support of her entire family. They have their work cut out for them, as they attend not only all the compulsory dressage shows for Carlotta but also the showjumping events for her two brothers.

Above *Carlotta Hassenbürger and Dulcia standing at attention while they play the German anthem at the European Pony Championships*
Opposite, top *Carlotta and Dulcia executing trot half-pass in the FEI Pony Team Test. All FEI tests from Pony to Grand Prix include this movement*
Opposite, bottom *Carlotta and Dulcia riding the Individual Pony test at the European Pony Championships in front of a large crowd. Temperatures that day were over 85 degrees*

Carlotta Hassenbürger

The Rider

My most memorable test

I will never forget the FEI European Pony Championships in Freudenberg in 2007, I had one of those perfect days, which was also my 14th birthday. Many of my friends and relatives came to support me and Dulcia at my first European Championships as I don't live far from Freudenberg. We made sure that we took time to enjoy the day. As it was my first year competing at this high level for ponies, I didn't think at all about winning but focused just on riding the best I could - I did not put pressure on myself.

Hours before I start to ride a test, I prepare by concentrating and thinking only about the test in question. The last thing I do is make sure my good luck charm is in my pocket, along with a special wooden medallion that my trainer gave to me.
At the Championships in Freudenberg, it had been a very warm day but half an hour before I was due to ride my test, it was raining cats and dogs and the whole arena was under water. Fortunately, unlike most other ponies, Dulcia doesn't mind the wet, in fact, she rather likes it, and she did a most wonderful test. It was a wonderful day anyway but it became a perfect day winning the Gold medal. Since then I feel I've grown up a lot and I've put pressure on myself to do well and strive for improvement.

My daily routine

I have to fit my riding in around school and all of my homework so I don't normally get to ride until late afternoon. Dulcia has a big window in her stable which I can see from my bedroom window so I can keep my eye on her. Besides riding and being an active member of the German Riding Association, I also do lots of swimming. Not all of my friends are riders so I feel I have a good balance in life. But when you are competing at this level there is not so much time left to do other things. There are certain competitions you must attend in order to make the National squads and with another FEI pony at home, my parents have a job managing our competition season, along with my brothers jumping competitions, but I prefer to have my life like this. When I am sixteen and am no longer allowed to compete on ponies, I intend to compete at the Junior level on a horse. I already have my horse which was competing at Grand Prix level in his younger life so he should find the movements easy in the Junior test. However, I haven't had much time to train on him while I am still training and competing Dulcia.

How my riding career began

I was born in Germany on the 20th July 1993 and started riding when I was only three years old, on a pony called Mendi. Mendi is a little mare just one metre high, but very intelligent. My two older brothers had started their riding careers on Mendi too. We still have her, she is over thirty years old now, and is still the boss in the yard. Instead of having her own stable she is allowed to wander around the entire farm and goes wherever she likes. People driving by often pull in to tell us there is a loose horse in our yard. As my family have been interested in horses for many generations, I was fortunate to have many ponies whilst I was growing up. My grandfather is a great supporter of all equestrian sports and, in fact, rode dressage ponies before the European Championships was even created. Both of my brothers are showjumpers.

I remember when I was six, riding Mendi at a show that I didn't do very well at. The judge spoke to me afterwards and told me that if I sat up straighter I would do much better. Although we had been out at

the show all day, when we got home, I took Mendi off the lorry and put her tack back on and started practising sitting up straighter. I have always been very determined. It isn't so much that I must win but I feel that I must do better each time and I will work very hard to achieve this. Before I turned nine years old I used to do lots of jumping and riding round our farm but after this point, I decided to ride dressage only. With my parents support and a pony like Dulcia I hope to learn as much as I can.

Cornelia Endres

The Trainer

Being Chef d' Equipe of the German Pony Dressage Squad

Since 1978, when the Pony European Championships first began, Germany has won Team gold 24 times, 18 of these consecutively and the German pony riders have taken the individual gold medal on 18 occasions, 10 of these consecutively. This dominating success is due to the legendary talents of the German Chef d'Equipe for the German pony dressage teams, Cornelia Endres who has held this Federal post for over 28 years.

I grew up and studied to become a sports teacher in Pirmasens, a small town in the Rhineland-Palatinate state near the French border. I have always loved riding particularly dressage and was our State Junior Dressage Champion three times and placed fourth in the German National Championships for Young Riders in 1969. After receiving my diploma for a sports coach, I became Head of the Youth Department of the German Riding Association in 1977. It was while I was running this department that I took over the care of the ponies, which led to my appointment as the Federal Trainer. I did enjoy competing myself, but I loved teaching more and eventually my teaching engagements took over and I was left with no time to ride. I also manage Gestüt Eulenhof, my riding and training facility, in Germany. When I am home I still ride everyday but I am not home that often.

  In Germany we are in a good position with our pony riders in that we have a good base of German bred ponies and a system in place for evaluating our up-and-coming riders. The ponies are there because we do not sell our best FEI dressage ponies. Instead we find other talented riders to take them over and offer them professional instruction and management. It is important to find good riders for the good ponies that their previous riders have outgrown and it would be a pity not to match up the good combinations based on the riders strength and physiodynamics. We start looking at ponies for the National squad throughout the winter months. We look at about 80 combinations which come to special clinics that we hold. From these we

Above *Cornelia Endres keenly watching German Pony Squad members during a training session at the European Pony Championships*
Opposite, top *Cornelia Endres on the podium with a happy German Pony squad who have just won Team Gold at the European Championships. This is Cornelia's 24th Team Gold medal as Chef d' Equipe*
Opposite, bottom *Cornelia putting the final touches Carlotta and Dulcia's warm up before they enter the arena*

My Story

1954 I was born on February 2nd in Pirmasens in Rhineland-Palatinate Germany.

1969 In dressage I placed 4th in the German National Championships.

1969 I graduated with a degree in sports coaching from a local college.

1977 I was appointed Head of the Youth Department of the German Riding Association.

1978 The National Federation appointed me as Federal Trainer of the ponies.

1978-2009 I was Chef d'Equipe for many Gold medal winning German Pony Dressage teams.

select 25 in the first official selection and from this we narrow it down to 10 in the second official selection. Then we nominate the few for the squad.

When I train or warm up the pony riders for competitions, I do it individually, so I need to know the pony and the child, as some children like to ride themselves and just need reassurance that what they are doing is good and some want to be told every step of the way.

Dulcia is the princess of the pony squad. She is very intelligent and very sensitive. Her mood changes from day to day, so sometimes you can push her harder than other days. It is important to know Dulcia so that you can train in the way that will give you the best results.

Dornik B is the professor. He is now older and has had many child riders. He knows exactly how to create his life so that he will have a long life. He does no more than he has to. He is not lazy but he likes to do the minimum. He does not need a lot of training anymore - the drills for half-pass etc. are not necessary. He loves to compete and puts all of his efforts into showing off.

Deinhard B started competing when he was very young. He was fresh, young and very, very charming. He made mistakes but the judges saw that he was charming and did not penalize him so much. But he needs a strict regime so that he does not get too spoiled or strong. He has to be educated very strictly so that he can be obedient. Sönke does a good job but Anna von Negri had fights with him - eventually Deinhard gave up arguing and became a great pony. Konrad is a completely different pony, he wants to know exactly what to do and he has an exact impression of what his life is. He knows precisely how to do things which makes him an excellent schoolmaster. The children must adapt to him, he does not adapt to them and when they do adapt to him, then they are riding correctly. Konrad has had five child riders already and they must know and tell him that he is the best. Once all of his needs are up to his standards, then he is ready to work in his way.

Dulcia

The Pony

Above *Dulcia and Carlotta in a training session between competitions. Carlotta rides every day in her quest to be the best pony rider*
Opposite, top *Carlotta's family, friends and groom congratulate her after a Gold medal winning ride on Dulcia. Families play an important role in the success of pony riders by acting as mentor, manager, financier and chauffeur. Without supportive families pony riders would find it very difficult to compete*

A day in the life

Dulcia is a palomino mare born in 1997 and I have had her for the last two seasons. She had competed at the top FEI European level before I got her, so she was used to all the attention and she thinks she is a bit like a princess. We have a special stable for our 7 ponies, which is separate from my brothers' jumping horses and stallions. In this stable block Dulcia always comes first. She has a very strict routine starting with breakfast at six-thirty in the morning. Once she has finished breakfast, she goes on the horse walker for about 10 to 15 minutes and then she is turned out in her paddock until about 11am, when she goes back to her stable for lunch. She has a rest after lunch and then is ridden or trained between about four and six in the evening. Once she has finished working she is put to bed and then later in the evening I pop out to check on her and give her an apple and a good night kiss. We try to make sure that everything is done on time so that Dulcia knows her daily routine. I believe that because she has such a strict routine, she is very calm and has never had colic or been lame. Dulcia likes other horses and ponies and she is always interested in what is going on around her especially when it comes to her food.

Dulcia's successful competition career started with her young owner, Lydia Camp. Together they won the German Bundeschampionate in 2001, 2002 and 2003 putting them in the same league as only two other German ponies, Dressmann and Dornick B. In 2003 they started their FEI dressage career winning the Gold Team medal and the Individual Bronze medal in their first European Championship held in Ireland. In 2006, their final year together, Lydia and Dulcia won Team Gold again and the Individual Gold medal. The FEI stipulates that riders can only compete on ponies in FEI events until the year in which they turn 16 years old. Lydia was already working with me on some of my other ponies but when she offered me the ride on Dulcia, I couldn't say no. Riding Dulcia has been a great introduction to international dressage.

Dulcia's Competition Highights

2000 1st Bundeschampionate with Katja Camp.

2001 1st Bundeschampionate, 1st German National Pony Champion with Lydia Camp.

2002 1st Bundeschampionate, German National Pony Champion with Lydia Camp.

2003 1st Bundeschampionate, 4th German Pony Champion, Team Gold, 3rd Individual Test at Pony European Championships Necarne Castle, Ireland, 4th Pony Preliminary, Team Gold, 3rd Individual at CDIO-P Freudenberg with Lydia Camp.

2004 5th Individual, Team Gold European Pony Championships Jaszkowo Poland, Team Gold at CDIO-P at Freudenberg, 2nd Preis der Besten Warendorf with Lydia Camp.

2006 1st Pony Preliminary Test and Individual Test, Team Gold European Pony Championships Saumur France, 4th Preis der Besten, Team Gold, 2nd Individual, 1st Kur at CDIP Touquet France, Team Gold 3rd Pony Preliminary and Individual at CDIP Aachen with Lydia Camp.

2007 Individual Silver, Team Gold at European Pony Championships Freudenburg Germany, 1st Pony Preliminary, Team and Individual Test at CDIP Addington GB, 4th Preis der Besten, 4th Pony Preliminary and Individual Test at CDIP Bonn, 3rd Pony Rider at German Youth Championships with Carlotta Hassenbürger.

2008 4th Pony Preliminary Test, Team Gold, 5th Individual at Pony European Championships Avenches, Switzerland, 3rd Preis der Besten with Carlotta Hassenbürger.

2009 1st Pony Preliminary at CDI Stadl Paura, 3rd Preis der Besten, 2nd Team Championship 4th Individual, 1st Kur at CDIO Saumur; 1st Team Championship, 4th Individual, 3rd Kur at CDI Stadl Paura Austria with Carlotta Hassenbürger.

Dulcia

Dulcia is a 147cm Rhinelander Palomino mare who was born in 1997. She was purchased by Lydia Camp who had a successful career in Pony dressage with Dulcia but has now been leased to Carlotta Hassenbürger until Carlotta turns 16 years old.

		Dandy
	Dancer	Valerina
Arts Dancer-Boy	Golden Charm	Valentino
		Goldina
Arts Demara	Derbino	Derby
		Valerina
	Kavalette	Kavalier
		Gundi

Above *A very excited Dulcia at the prize-giving victory lap for the Team test in which she won the Gold medal. Carlotta has to use all of her strength to keep Dulcia under control*

Pony Collected Trot

Sanneke Rothenberger and Konrad

The pony, remaining 'on the bit' moves forward with his neck raised and arched. The hocks, being well engaged, maintain an energetic impulsion, thus enabling the shoulders to move with greater ease in any direction. The pony's steps are shorter than in the other trots, but he is lighter and more mobile.

Here we see the talented Sanneke Rothenberger on her pony Konrad. Although the neck itself could perhaps be longer, the activity from the well-flexed joints of the hind leg is obvious, as is the lightness and mobility of the shoulder, thereby producing this lovely picture of cadence and expression within the trot strides. The rider is sitting well in the saddle with an upright, yet supple position, which enables her to be effective and independent, allowing her to absorb the movement of her pony whilst appearing to remain still and elegant in her posture.

The development of a good riding position and seat early on in your riding career is essential if you want to be an effective rider regardless of what level of dressage you compete at. Just as horses need to develop their muscles for strength and purpose as they advance from the simpler movements toward the more difficult movements so too must the rider keep themselves fit and capable both physically and mentally to perform these movements without letting their physical or mental inefficiencies interfere with the horse's abilities. The rider should be able to enhance the development of the horse not hinder it and a well developed correct seat and position will go a long way to ensure this. In Sanneke's case she has had the advantage of learning the correct position and seat from very early days as both her parents are accomplished Grand Prix riders and are heavily involved with her training. The result of

these good practices can be seen in Sanneke's ability to perform at the top of her league in ponies and then to transfer and improve on these riding skills in the move up to horses where she went on to win three Gold medals at the European Junior Dressage Championships in 2009. A very rare feat in such a competitive sport.

However, as good as a rider may be their talents must be combined with the talents of a very good pony to ensure success in the show ring. The German Pony Dressage team was very fortunate to have had at their disposal an excellent selection of ponies whose natural abilities were such that they were able to supply Germany with an almost endless array of Gold medals over a period of twenty years. Careful breeding and the insight of a very clever chef d'equipe with the ability to match the right child with the right pony was instrumental to Germany's success. Konrad was the epitome of the perfect dressage pony, - excellent paces, self-motivated, and easy enough to ride that a child could execute the most beautiful movements on him. Konrad had five child riders during his competitive dressage career and his last rider, the very talented Sanneke Rothenberger, continued his winning form until his retirement in 2008. Having been managed by children all of his life, Konrad will still have the opportunity to do what he has always loved and that is to teach young children but at home.

Sanneke Rothenberger

The Rider

My daily routine

On the days that I am competing in the morning, I like to be up at least three hours before my test. If it is an afternoon, I like to stay in my hotel or caravan as late as possible, as I don't like to see anyone before I compete. I spend this quiet time preparing myself mentally - how I should train him, how I should ride and how I should present him in the test. I go with the groom to get Konrad ready, normally feeding him lots of carrots and apples. I then walk the test accurately in the stable before getting on him about 30 minutes before the test to warm him up. I always have to wear my special lucky charms, which include my watch, necklace and earrings. If I don't remember them, I get panicky.

If I get nervous before a pony test, my mother teases me that I have already ridden Grand Prix - as she was pregnant with me when she was competing in Grand Prix - so I have nothing to be nervous about.

I was fortunate to have grown up in a family that loves horses. We have ponies of all sizes on our farm. When I was four I was able to ride without a saddle but I didn't start training for dressage until I was nine years old. I ride immediately after school so that I have time to do other things in the evening.

In my last year of ponies I had to make the decision to ride ponies or horses, in fact I couldn't make the decision, I had to let my mother make it for me because it was too hard. I had always wanted to win a European Gold medal on Konrad and did not want to give up the ride until I did. My mother reminded me that we have won Gold medals at the Nationals and other FEI events and Konrad will not know if it was the Europeans or another event that he won it at. I was already leading the Junior division on my horse Paso Doble. In the end I decided to ride in the Junior division and I won the Team Gold medal, the Individual Gold medal and the Gold medal for the Kur, I could not have dreamed of so many successes.

I cannot see myself not riding but I do not want to do it professionally only as an amateur. My plan is that I would like to be a business women, something to do with management, as I am very organised like my father. When I rode Konrad at the CDIP at Addington in England, we went to visit Cambridge University. This is where I would love to study. At home I ride more advanced movements, as we always train at a little more advanced level to make the pony tests easier. But we

My Competition Highlights

2004 4th Z2 D/E and 2nd Z2 D/E on Domino Dancing at CDI-P Beek Netherlands.

2005 1st Pony Team Test 4th Individual Test at Weert on Domino Dancing.

2006 3rd Pony Team Test 4th Test D-ZII on Domino Dancing 2nd Junior Team Test 2nd Kur on Paso Doble at CDN-PJYR Weert, 3rd Pony Preliminary and Team Test on Dino P 1st Junior Team Individual and Kur test on Paso Doble at CDI-PJYR Weikersdorf Austria, 1st Pony Preliminary Test 4th Team Test 2nd Individual Test on Dino P at CDI-PJYR Stadl Paura Austria, 2nd Hessian PDB Test 1 and 2 at Preis der Besten on Dino P.

2007 1st Junior Team Championship Test 3rd Junior Individual Test at CDI Weert on Wembley, 3rd Junior Championship Test 1st Junior Individual Test at CDI Weert on Paso Doble 5th Pony Team and Individual Tests at CDI-PJYR Neubeeren.

2008 3rd Junior Riders Preis der Besten, 1st Team Individual Test and Kur Junior European Championships Azeitao Portugal on Paso Doble.

2009 Gold Team medal Gold Individual and Gold Kur on Deveraux Old at European Junior Championships at Ermelo Holland, 1st Team Test 1st Individual and 1st Kur on Paso Doble at German Youth Riders Championships at Munich Germany.

don't teach the flying change. Konrad has never done a flying change but he does half-pass in canter, pirouettes and pirouettes in canter. My parents use their experiences having ridden Grand Prix on many horses to help me train my pony in the best way possible. We always talk in the evening discussing the way the horses go and what the plan will be for the next day. We are always talking about horses. Growing up with such competitive family members means life can be hectic sometimes. In 2005 I was competing Konrad on the German team in Italy at the Pony European Championships while at the same time my father was competing for Holland at the European Championships in Hagen, Germany. My mother came with me to help me and cheer on the German team while at the same supporting my father on the Dutch team. In 2007, my brother and I were both on the German team at the Pony European Championships and we won the Team Gold medal, making it a proud day for my parents. What was more unusual about that day was that my cousin who was riding for the Dutch team won the Silver medal making it a very proud day for my grandparents who were watching.

Opposite *Sanneke and Konrad winning the Preis de Besten 2008*
Above *Sanneke and Konrad in extended trot at the CDIP at Addington UK*
Right *Sanneke at the European Pony Championships 2008, waving a banner in honour of her brother Sönke who had just won the Individual Gold medal*

Gonnelien Rothenberger -Gordijn

The Trainer

Training Sanneke and Konrad

Konrad has had a fortunate life in that he has always been in good hands from the start - a good pony always comes with good riding. Connie Endres, the pony Chef d' Equipe, is very good at matching a good pony with a good rider. Connie knows all of the good ponies in Germany and as we had always trained with her she could make a good match. He was much heavier when he first arrived and he has lost about 30kg and looks much lighter, like an athlete, but we have to watch his diet as he loves to eat everything. This is the only thing we changed about Konrad. I learned from Sven to watch and learn how the pony was trained because this is what has made the pony so good.

When we decided to buy him we watched how he was ridden so that we could do the same to him when Sanneke rode him. We even bought his saddle and bridle so that nothing had to change. Konrad is still ridden in the same saddle and bridle as when he was 6 years old. I never tried to change his training. I never assumed that I knew everything because I rode Grand Prix. After Konrad was with us for a year we improved on a few things but never retraining.

Sanneke for her age is a very sensitive rider, she feels so much. There was one time when Konrad was lame and Sanneke felt instantly that he was not right. No one else could see it but she could tell that he was not with her like he normally would be. Sure enough he did come lame later. Sanneke was only thirteen when she felt this. It makes it easier for a coach or trainer to work with someone like this because they can communicate these feelings to you, so you can help them more. I can teach and tell the rider what to do but I can't train feeling. Sanneke has a good way of riding, she would not just ride the shoulder-in technically, for instance, she would ride the shoulder-in with feeling.

Konrad rides like a German horse. In my opinion he is almost perfect but he has an open mind so when things happen out of the ordinary such as noisy photographers' cameras he can get nervous. Not that anyone on the ground could see it but Sanneke can feel it. Konrad gives the feeling one would expect to feel from a horse. You don't have to kick him and you don't

My Story

1968 I was born June 5th in Weert, Limburg, Netherlands.

1976 At the age of eight I began to ride.

1983/4 I represented Holland at the European Pony Championships in Sweden and then France.

1989 I moved to Germany to train with Conrad Schumacher and Ellen Bontje.

2002 After competing in the Dutch Indoor Championships I decided to retire from active competition and focus on helping my children to ride and compete.

Gonnelien's Competition Highlights

1996 Team silver at Atlanta Olympics on Olympic Bo (Dondolo).

1998 19th Grand Prix 16th Special at World Equestrian Games Rome on Dondolo.

2000 2nd Grand Prix 1st Kur at CDI Ebreichsdorf on Leonardo da Vinci.

2001 1st Dutch National Dressage Championships 3rd Grand Prix 2nd Kur

CDI-W at Neumunster on Weyden, 3rd Grand Prix 2nd Kur CDI-W Berlin, 2nd overall in Western League standing for World Cup on Leonardo da Vinci, 4th Grand Prix 1st Special CDI Arnham on Jonggor's Weyden.

2002 8th Grand Prix 9th Special 7th Kur on Leonardo da Vinci and 13th Grand Prix 10th Special on C'est Bon at Dutch Dressage Championships, 5th World Cup Final on Leonardo da Vinci. 14th World Equestrian Games in Jerez de la Frontera on Weyden, 3rd Grand Prix CDI-W Maastricht on Barclay II.

have to pull him. Only a few children would have had the privilege to ride a pony with such a feeling. This, I think, is part of the reason that Sanneke was able to go up to horses so early.

When we are at competition we start long with the walk then the trot and then with canter transitions to get his back swinging. She rides the canter first in a jumping position to free the back. We do everything to make the pony happy and relaxed at a show. We don't use the show to win using tricks or coverups. We manage to the point that we show only the results of the training that we do at home. Konrad is so motivated that we only need at most 40 minutes to warm up. If the warm-up was longer he would just be on his toes even more to get going, and if he was like that he would be too difficult for a child to ride because he would just want to give everything. We do lots of walks to make him think there is no show. Sometimes we even have cold starts to make him think there is no competition and to relax him.

Above and left *Gonnelien and Dondolo at the World Equestrian Games in Rome 1998*
Opposite *Gonnelien an accomplished Grand Prix rider does not compete so much these days so she can spend more time teaching her children the art of dressage*

Konrad

The Pony

A day in the life

Konrad is a 147cm high, Weser Ems gelding, a famous son of the famous Welsh Pony stallion, Constanin. He is one of Germany's most successful dressage ponies, if not *the* most successful.

Konrad does not get along with many horses or ponies but they all seem to love him. When he comes in to his stable, the others whinny to him but he ignores them - he is only interested in his food. He wants to be quiet and he wants to be in his box and eat and he wants to be ridden. This is about as complicated as he wants his life to be. Konrad doesn't like us to go on holidays because he has to go in the horse walker and he would rather be ridden. His mood changes and he becomes grumpy. He loves to be ridden by children and gets so excited when we start to groom him to get him ready. He can't tell me if he is really happy but he does look

Above *Sanneke and Konrad at the European Pony Championships held at Freudenberg, Germany*
Right *Staying warm at the CDIP at Addington UK with help from her father Sven. Once Konrad completes his test his protective boots go back on and he is covered with a warm rug to protect him against the cold damp weather in England*
Opposite *Sanneke and Konrad on their way to victory in the Pony Team Test*

Konrad's Competition Highlights

1994 German Dressage Champion for four year olds.

1996 German Dressage Champion for six year olds.

1997 1st Individual and Team Gold at Pony European Championships at Hartpury UK with Nikolas Kröncke

1999 Gold medal Preliminary Test, Team and Individual Test at Pony European Championships Stromsholm, Sweden with Kira Kröncke.

2000 6th Preliminary Test, Team Gold, 3rd Individual Test at European Pony Championships at Hagen with Kira Kröncke.

2001 3rd Preliminary Test, Team Gold, 4th Individual, 2nd Preliminary test, 4th Individual at European Pony Champions at Vejer de la Frontera with Annika Fiege.

2002 1st Preliminary Test, Team Gold, 2nd Individual Test at European Pony Championships Hagen, 2nd Preis der Besten with Annika Fiege.

2003 2nd Preliminary test, Gold Team medal, 2nd Individual test at European Pony Championships Irvinestown, Ireland, 3rd Preis der Besten in Germany, !st German Championships with Patricia Hohn.

2004 3rd Preliminary Test, Team Gold, 3rd Individual Test at Pony European Championships Jaszkowo, Poland, 4th Preis der Besten Germany with Patricia Hohn.

2005 2nd Preliminary Test, Team Gold, 2nd Individual at European Pony Championships Pratoni del Vivaro, Italy, 2nd Preliminary Test, 1st Team Test, 1st Individual Test Freudenberg, 2nd Pony Team, 1st Individual Test at CDN Weert with Sanneke Rothenberger.

2006 2nd Preliminary Test, Team Gold, Individual Finals at European Pony Championships Saumur, 2nd Preis der Besten, 1st Pony Team Test, 1st Pony Test D-ZII at CDN-PJYR Weert, 1st Pony Preliminary Test, 1st Pony Team Test, 1st Individual Test at CDI-PJYR Weikersdorf, Austria, 1st Hessian PDB Test 1 and 2 at Preis der Besten with Sanneke Rothenberger.

2007 3rd Preliminary Test, Team Gold, 1st Consolation Finals at Pony European Championships Freudenberg, 2nd German Pony Championships, 1st Pony Riders Preis der Besten, 1st Preliminary Test and Individual Test at CDI Weert Holland, 2nd Pony Team and Individual tests at CDI-PJYR Neubeeren, 3rd Pony Preliminary, 2nd Team and Individual tests at CDI-P Bonn with Sanneke Rothenberger.

2008 1st Pony Riders Preis der Besten with Sanneke Rothenberger.

forward to being ridden and I take this as a sign that he still wants to go on for a while longer. He is now 19 years old and my younger sister will train on him at home but he will no longer go to competitions.

Konrad loves sugar, apples, bananas and most things to do with food. He is turned out in his little field every day after I ride him. When he first arrived at our stables when he was turned out, he would run and run. My grandfather had to build a smaller paddock for him so he would be calmer and not gallop all over the place.

Konrad's successful ridden career started with the Kröncke family. When he was seven, he was competed by Nikolas Kröncke and then when he was nine, Nikolas' sister, Kira, rode him. When he was twelve years old, he was campaigned by Annika Fiege followed by Patricia Hohn, when he was 13 and 14 years old. For the past five years he has been in our stables. All of the children who have ridden Konrad have won many gold medals on him. It is such a testament to his superb way of going, his easy rideability and his desire to compete over so many years. I feel very fortunate to have started my riding career on such a great pony.

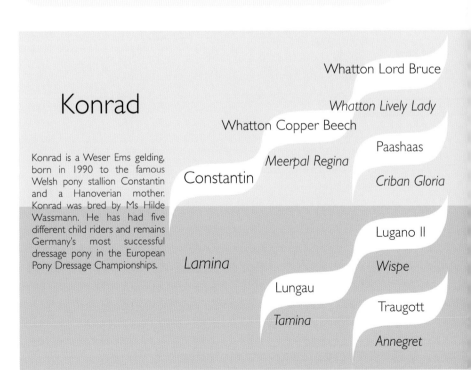

Konrad

Konrad is a Weser Ems gelding, born in 1990 to the famous Welsh pony stallion Constantin and a Hanoverian mother. Konrad was bred by Ms Hilde Wassmann. He has had five different child riders and remains Germany's most successful dressage pony in the European Pony Dressage Championships.

Constantin
  Whatton Copper Beech
    Whatton Lord Bruce
    Whatton Lively Lady
  Meerpal Regina
    Paashaas
    Criban Gloria

Lamina
  Lungau
    Lugano II
    Wispe
  Tamina
    Traugott
    Annegret

Glossary

'On The Bit' When the horse carries his head in a near vertical position and he is calmly accepting the rider's contact on the reins.

BD British Dressage.

Broodmare Female horse used for breeding.

Bundeschampionate German young horse and pony championships where 3 to 6 year old German bred horses and ponies compete to be the champions in the riding horse, dressage horse, jumping horse, event horse, driving horse, riding pony, dressage pony, event pony, and the jumping pony classes.

Cadence A word derived from rhythm and flow. The marked accentuation of the tempo arising from the spring and elasticity of the horse.

Carriage, self carriage When the horse moves in a correct and balanced frame without relying on the rider to 'hold' this balance. Occasionally referred to as the horses 'posture'.

CDI Concours de Dressage International- An International calibre dressage competition under FEI rules. Occasionally followed by the letters P, J and YR meaning Pony riders, Junior riders and Young riders. These are classes of competition which differ in age of rider and level of dressage.

CDI3* A conventional international competition open to a select number of countries.

CDI5* World Dressage Masters competition.

CDIO International team competition.

CDI-W World Cup Qualifier.

CDN A National Competition.

Chef d'Equipe Usually an individual person who is responsible for the coordination and representation of their teams or individuals at international competitions. They must attend all the technical meetings which are held at international competitions and are first and foremost part of team management.

CHIO Concours Hippique International Officiel.

Colic Abdominal pain in the horse's stomach that can encompass all gastrointestinal conditions. There are a variety of causes and some which can be fatal without surgical intervention.

Collection of the horse The opposite of extension- Where the rider, by means of carefully balanced driving and restraining aids, causes the horse's frame to become more compact and the horse light and supple in the hand. The baseline is shortened, the croup is lowered, the shoulder is raised and the head is held on the vertical thus increasing the ability of the horse to lower and engage its quarters.

Conformation The degree of correctness of a horse's bone structure, musculature, and its body proportions in relation to each other. The ability to perform a specific task could be limited by a horse's undesirable conformation, although this would depend on the form to function trait.

Elasticity The ability or tendency to stretch and contract the musculature smoothly, giving the impression of stretchiness or springiness.

Elevated The raising of the head and neck (including the base of the neck) freely from lifted withers. Can also be applied in piaffe and passage to address the height to which forelegs are raised.

Engaged The hind legs are engaged when they are brought well under the body.

European Championships (Dressage) A competition held every other year for seniors and every year for Ponies, Juniors, Young Riders in Europe in which each European country may send a team of four to compete in each level.

Eventing an equestrian event which comprises dressage, cross-country and show-jumping. This event has its roots as a comprehensive cavalry test. It usually takes place in the format of a one day event, two day or three day event.

FEI Federation Equestre International- The international governing body of equestrian sports. It recognises 10 disciplines: dressage, eventing, horseball, endurance riding, combined driving, Para-equestrianism, reining, show-jumping, vaulting and tent pegging.

FEI Coupes des Ameriques Championship of the Americas under FEI rules and regulations.

FEI Dressage Commission The Dressage branch of the FEI. For more information please go to www.fei.org/Disciplines/Dressage/Pages/Default.aspx

Footfall The way and order a horses feet fall which is different for each pace and gait.

Forehand A horse may be considered 'on the forehand' if it leaves the weight on the forefeet too long (picks up the front feet too late in the stride.)

Freestyle see Kur

Gaits The different ways a horse can move. The standard natural gaits or paces are: walk, trot, canter and gallop. There are also bred or trained additional gaits: pacing, ambling, running walk. A horse can only do one gait at a time.

Gelding A castrated male horse.

Gestüt German word meaning stud.

Girth A strap encircling the horse's body to secure the saddle to its back.

Grand Prix The highest level of competitive dressage. It is a test used to determine team medals at an International competition and the first round of the Individual competition such as the Olympics and the World Equestrian Games.

Grand Prix Special A test that uses the same movements as the Grand Prix (see above) but in a more difficult sequence. This test is also used as the second round of the Individual event at an International competition such as the Olympics.

Groom The person who carries out the grooming of the horse, but may also look after all of its needs such as feeding, and cleaning the stable.

Ground Jury This is made up of five judges who will judge the competition in a specific class.

Half-halt A hardly visible, coordinated action of the seat, legs and hand of the rider resulting in a momentary increase in collection used to enhance the horses balance, lightness of the forehand and attention before the execution of a movement or transition.

Hand-grazed This is when a horse is allowed to graze or eat grass while being held and controlled by a person, usually a groom using a lunge or lead rope.

Hanoverian A warmblood horse originating in Germany. It is one of the oldest, most numerous, and most successful of the warmbloods.

Hock The 'knee' of a horse's hind leg.

Horse Walker An exercise machine where the horses walk in a circle. Large ones enable the horses to trot and even canter around the circle.

IPS A Dutch horse group which sponsors many top dressage combinations including Anky van Grunsven on IPS Salinero and IPS Painted Black. For more information go to www.ipshorsegroup.nl/en/

Impulsion The horses desire to carry and move itself forward. Release of the energy stored by engagement. In dressage, impulsion is associated with a phase of suspension such as exists in trot and canter.

Intermediate I and II A high level of dressage test. International Dressage Riders Club- represents the interests of all dressage riders particularly those taking part in FEI international competitions. For more information visit www.idrc.me

International Dressage Trainers Club Promotes correct dressage training and strives to encourage dressage riding worldwide. Members are professionals who have trained riders competing at Grand Prix or Pony/Junior /Young riders. For more information visit www.idtc-online.com.

Kur A freestyle dressage test that is ridden to music.

KWPN The Royal Warmblood Studbook of the Netherlands

Lame or lameness A condition in which a horse does not carry weight equally on all four legs, due to disease or injury.

Lightness This refers to the horse's lightness on its feet, the lightness in the reins. It is also a component of 'self carriage.'

Liveries People who pay for the upkeep of their horses on someone else's property.

Lunge or lunging A technique for training or exercising horses, where a horse is asked to work at the end of a long line and respond to commands from a handler on the ground who holds the line. It is also a critical component of the sport of equestrian vaulting.

Mare A female horse

Moment of Suspension When all four of the horses feet are off the ground at the same time.

One and Two Tempi Changes Multiple flying changes strung together to form a movement in a Grand Prix test. In a one tempi the horse changes leg every stride, a two tempi - every other stride and so on.

Paces Any variation within a gait, such as collected or extended in walk, trot and canter.

Pan American Games A multi-sport event, held every four years in the year before the Olympic Games and between competitors from all nations in the Americas.

Poll The part of the horse's head that is just behind or between the two ears.

Preis der Besten A mid-season evaluation championship of the current show level of the German Pony, Junior and Young Riders. It is an important selection trial for these German teams held early in the competitive season.
Prix St Georges An internationally recognised level of dressage test.

Reining A western riding competition for horses where the riders guide the horses through a precise pattern of circles, spins, and stops. Reining is often described as a Western form of dressage riding, as it requires the horse to be responsive and in tune with its rider, whose aids should not be easily seen, and judges the horse on its ability to perform a set pattern of movements.

Saddle A supportive structure for a rider that is secured to the horses back by a girth. They are usually specialized depending on the particular sport the horse is used for.

Schoolmaster A horse with the experience and the ability to help a rider learn and perfect certain skills.

Seat ie the rider's seat. This is where the rider supports their weight on the horse, such as the riders sitting bones. Is also viewed as a connection between the horse and rider and so an aid in performing movements and transitions.

Self-carriage see Carriage

Serpentine A series of half-circles connected by a straight line over the centre line.

Spanish Riding School of Vienna A centre for classical dressage in Austria, famous for its Lipizzaner horses.

Spurs Metal riding aids with a shank of the back of the heel pointing towards the rear, worn as a pair and secured to the rider's ankle by a strap.

Stallion An uncastrated male horse.

Stallion Testing Either a 30-day 'suitability test', or a 'station test' of 70 - Days, 100 - Days or 300 - Days of tests to fulfill a stallion's performance requirements. A stallion that attends the suitability test must perform at an age-appropriate level in open competition to complete his requirements. The suitability test must be combined with a performance record in order to fulfill a stallion's performance requirement.

Stride The cycle of movements that is completed when the horse's legs regain their initial positions.

Tacked up A horse is said to be tacked up when the riding equipment or tack, such as a saddle and bridle, has been put on the horse so that it is ready to be ridden.

Thoroughbred A horse breed that is best known for its use in racing whose lineage can be traced back to three specific Arabian stallion of the 1600's, Godolphin Barb, Byerly Turk and Darley Arabian.

Trakehner Considered one of the lightest and most refined warmblood horse breeds. The name derives from Trakehnen, the site of the Main Stud (Gestüt Trakehnen) in Prussia.

Transition The process of moving from one gait or pace to another or from one variation of gait or pace to another.

Travers The horse is slightly bent around the inside leg of the rider, and looking in the direction it is going. It's outside legs pass and cross in front of the inside legs.

Uphill Referring to the horse's longitudinal balance: higher in the forehand, relative to the croup.

USEF United States Equestrian Federation for more information visit www.usef.org.

Vaulting An equestrian sport involving gymnastic exercises done on the back of a moving horse.

Warmblood Middle-weight breeds of horses mainly used for equestrian sport.

WEG World Equestrian Games

Weser Ems Also known as a Deutsche Reitpony is a German breed of pony. It is often described as a 'miniature warmblood' with refined, horse-like characteristics that make it suitable as a children's pony and also as a mount for sport horse competition in Europe.

Westphalian A warmblood horse bred in the Westphalia region of western Germany. Since World War II, the Westphalian horse has been bred to the same standard as the other German warmbloods, and they are particularly famous as Olympic-level show jumpers and dressage horses.

Whinnying The sound a horse makes to communicate.

World Cup Final and Qualifiers An FEI regulated competition held yearly. Combinations must qualify in their region, with the top combinations being invited to the final which can be held anywhere in the world.

Photographic Credits

All photographs and illustrations are the sole property and copyright of LewisHarding Ltd unless stated otherwise below.

Index

Page numbers in *italic* refer to the illustrations

Photograph opposite:
Edward Gal and
Moorlands Totilas after
smashing another World
Record at the European
Championships 2009.